SHISENDO

S H I S E N D O
Hall of the Poetry Immortals

by J. Thomas Rimer, Jonathan Chaves,
Stephen Addiss, and Hiroyuki Suzuki

New York   WEATHERHILL   Tokyo

First edition, 1991

Published by Weatherhill, Inc., 420 Madison Avenue, 15th Fl.,
New York, New York 10017, and Tanko-Weatherhill, 8-3
Nibancho, Chiyoda-ku, Tokyo 102. Protected by copyright
under terms of the International Copyright Union; all rights
reserved. Printed in Japan.

Library of Congress Cataloging in Publication Data:

Shisendo, hall of the poetry immortals / by J. Thomas Rimer
. . . [et al.].–1st ed.
      p.   cm.
  Includes bibliographical references.
  ISBN 0-8348-0241-4 (pbk.) : $29.95
  1. Ishikawa, Jōzan, 1583–1672—Criticism and
  interpretation.
I. Rimer, J. Thomas.
PL795.I74Z87   1991
895.6'132–dc20
                                      91-22217
                                           CIP

Contents

"My retreat in Vaucluse is a most favorable place for my studies; hills cast their shadows both in the morning and in the evening; there are sudden hidden nooks; there is everywhere a tranquil solitude, wherein you see the footprints of beasts oftener than those of men; and there is a perpetual silence, broken only by the murmuring of the swiftly flowing stream, the lowing of the cattle pastured on its banks, and the singing of birds. I could say more, were it not that because of the rare gifts bestowed by nature on this place, it is already known far and wide through my verses."

—the poet Petrarch, 1347

"Today I went to the Shisendō. It is said that the rooms and gardens alike were designed by Ishikawa Jōzan. Sections of the construction from that time remain, and a nun now looks after them. The place is small, yet what one sees is of real grandeur. The whole place is filled with a poetic spirit, yet without any hint of a sentimental flourish; every detail is held in perfect balance.

It is spots such as these which represent for us Europeans a whole new dimension in Japanese art. How to express it? Perhaps one might say something like this—here 'art lies in just the things we overlook in art.' The gardens are put together with only groups of trees, grasses, and stones. There is nothing more; indeed, if there were no pond, it might appear as though there were nothing artistic about the place at all. Yet the atmosphere engendered represents something higher than simple nature itself. Could it be said to represent a sort of means towards self-contemplation, at the same time transparent and humble? In any case, I have finally come to know what is the highest of all the Japanese artistic achievements. These gardens stand alone among the masterpieces created in the various Japanese arts. Indeed, there is nothing like them in the world."

—the architect Bruno Taut, 1936

Foreword

J. Thomas Rimer

The temptation to think in prescribed categories is such an overwhelming one that we scarcely notice our unarticulated commitment to doing so. Looking at other civilizations and other periods in history helps us break down those barriers and limitations in order to sense buried connections that enrich each other. In no area of artistic and cultural history is an understanding of such connections so necessary, and so exciting, as in the case of the arts of Japan's Tokugawa period. In this rich cultural period, a long era of relative political tranquillity from 1600 to 1867, a synthetic vision of the arts developed that was quite remarkable. Painters wrote poetry, poets designed architecture, architects planned gardens. Each artistic form existed and defined itself in larger contexts; no one of them can be properly studied or appreciated in isolation.

The Shisendō is a lovely and relatively isolated residence of a samurai turned recluse, Ishikawa Jōzan (1583–1672). Now a Buddhist temple of the Sōto sect of Zen, the Shisendō was built by Jōzan in 1641 on a hilly slope that lies in the northeast suburbs of Kyoto. For many reasons, the Shisendō provides an extraordinarily appropriate environment in which to observe these artistic linkages as they functioned together to reinforce each other.

Geography produces differences in cultures; time also creates still another sense of mystery and distance—in the case of the Shisendō, as much for contemporary Japanese visitors as for visitors from abroad. To convey something of the attitudes of mind that allowed Jōzan to construct his environment, we felt that no single scholar or writer could encompass all aspects of his subtle and holistic vision. What is more, Jōzan's viewpoint is such a personal one that each contributor found himself addressing his topic from a highly individual point of view. In that regard, our essays overlap; normal scholarly boundaries touch, then flow together. Such shifting enthusiasms are also Jōzan's legacy to us; and, capturing something of his eclectic spirit, Jōzan's example helped us, with our different enthusiasms, collaborate on this book.

In addition to the contributors to the volume, there are many others to thank in what has been, modest as it is, an undertaking of some years. We are extremely grateful to the publisher Benridō of Kyoto for kind permission to reprint many of the photographs from the lavish volume *Shisendō*, edited by Takudo Ishikawa, the chief priest of the temple when the work was published in Kyoto in 1971 on the occasion of the three-hundredth anniversary of the building of Jōzan's villa.* And we want to pay special tribute to his son, Ishikawa Junshi, the present chief priest, whose graciousness and support of this project is deeply appreciated. We would like to thank Joseph Seubert, now resident in Japan, who helped provide us with written materials on Jōzan, both published and unpublished, from the Tokugawa and the modern periods, many of them extremely difficult to find. Mrs. Fumi Norica at the Library of Congress in Washington located materials in this country, provided the quotation from Bruno Taut, and made a number of wise suggestions about the volume. We appreciate Shūichi Katō's permission to reprint his short story, "The Hall of the Poetry Immortals," in a translation first published under the title "The Pavilion of Great Poets" in the *Japan Quarterly*, vol. XIII, no. 4, October–December, 1966. Finally, we want to thank Weatherhill's editor-in-chief Jeffrey Hunter and his gifted designers and staff for their care, enthusiasm, and talent in assembling all the elements that have gone into the making of this beautiful book.

*Japanese names are given in Western order—given name followed by family name—for those born after 1868 and in traditional order—family name followed by given name—for those born earlier.

SHISENDO

Ishikawa Jōzan

J. Thomas Rimer

I

I suppose that something of my own habits of mind is revealed in the fact that my first attraction to Ishikawa Jōzan started with a sentence or two I read about Kyoto. Many years ago, when I first began to read works of Japanese literature in translation, I found myself fascinated, as have been so many others, by the descriptions of an elegant traditional house in the old capital that serves as a setting for the peculiar events that transpire in Jun'ichirō Tanizaki's short novel *The Bridge of Dreams* (1959). Among the objects that gave distinction to the garden of that house was a water mortar that sounded continuously.

> Even today, the sound of a water mortar echoes through the garden of the Hall of Poets, the home of the early Edo poet Ishikawa Jōzan in the northern suburbs of Kyoto. There, too, is displayed an explanatory text written in Chinese by Jōzan. I suppose the reason why we had a water mortar is that my grandfather went there, read the description and got the impulse to copy the device in his own house. It is said that Jōzan's poem about not wishing to cross the Kamo River was written as a polite way of declining an invitation from the Emperor:
>
> > Alas, I am ashamed to cross it—
> > Though only a shallow stream
> > It would mirror my wrinkled age.
>
> A rubbing of the poem hangs in the alcove in the Hall of Poets, and we had one at our house too.[1]

---

1. Jun'ichirō Tanizaki, *Seven Japanese Tales,* translated by Howard Hibbett (New York: Knopf, 1963, reprinted Putnam, 1981), 101–2.

This was all that Tanizaki wrote about Jōzan. I found the clues intriguing.

I knew nothing then about the art of calligraphy, and the fact that a work of calligraphy in a room could both suggest the personality of its creator and dignify its surroundings excited my curiosity. No book in my small library of studies on Japanese art included any mention of Ishikawa Jōzan. I dropped the whole matter, but my curiosity remained unfulfilled.

My initial fascination was strongly renewed when, some fifteen years later, I was advised by a Japanese architect friend to visit the Shisendō, that "Hall of Poets," or, more properly, the "Hall of the Poetry Immortals," mentioned in Tanizaki's story. "The house and garden were built by a wonderful eccentric poet and calligrapher named Ishikawa Jōzan," he told me. "It is one of the most private and perfect places in the whole city, and you must see it in order to get a sense of one whole side of elegant Japanese culture."

Shisendō is certainly famous now. Busloads of curious schoolchildren tramp dutifully through its tiny rooms and perfectly proportioned garden spaces, displaying a disturbing energy that might well threaten the foundations of Versailles, let alone those of this series of slight, fragile pavilions built of straw and wood. A decade or more ago, however, such was not the case. Indeed, the Shisendō was not even listed in that Baedeker-by-any-other-name, the Japan Travel Bureau's Official Guide to Japan, long familiar to all foreign travelers with an interest in Japanese culture, but had remained a special footnote, its details known only to the discerning few.

After making a series of inquiries and riding, as I recall, an embarrassing number of streetcars and buses, I managed to reach the bottom of the hillside tucked away in the northeast corner of Kyoto where the building and its gardens stood in relative isolation. A walk up the hill brought the sight of a brushwood gate, which I ducked through. Soon, obligatory ticket and souvenir postcards in hand, I entered the refined world of Jōzan.

It is impossible, of course, to know if the building and gardens remain precisely as they were when they were constructed around 1641, but they appear as if they might be the same. A small antechamber leads into a large, matted room open to the garden on three sides. Portraits of thirty-six classical Chinese poets admired by Jōzan are hung just under the ceiling of the room.

The effect is both aristocratic and rustic. From the room, which serves as a kind of terrace, the eye can move out toward the small garden of oval and oblong plantings that drop cunningly down the hill to a screen of bushes and trees that allow the city below to appear, if at all, through a haze of green. Moss nestled on the hillsides is juxtaposed with tall grasses and flowering trees. Halfway down there is a pond and, beside it, a small detached pavilion. Looking back up at the house from that point you can see an elegant moon-viewing turret with a curved window that forms a kind of second story over the main room above.

It can be said, I suppose, that the garden and the house, taken together, do not quite represent the art that conceals art, a quality that some Japanese gardens possess. The shapes, the juxtapositions are occasionally a bit too idiosyncratic, the space a little too small for the tricks of perspective to play themselves out in full. Yet my own perceptions, correct or not, made the Hall of the Poetry Immortals all the more endearing to me, for the total effect suggested a place and an image quite in consonance with the one I was beginning to form of the man himself.

I have since made many trips to the Shisendō. Indeed, I go there every time I visit Kyoto. Some things have changed, of course. Parking spaces have been added. The colors on the postcards are brighter. There is even an automatic hundred-yen drink-dispensing machine (fruit juice, Coca-Cola, and beer, as I recall) not far from the entrance, to assuage the thirst of all of those who make the climb. Still, the atmosphere of the place remains as enchanting and as elusive as always. I have tried to learn something about the Shisendō and the man who built it. I have read what there is to know, but it is not enough. There is still a gap, a kind of pause in our modern understanding. Indeed, it has occurred to me that with our own cultural preferences for certain kinds of knowledge we may seek to know the wrong things about Jōzan; or if not wrong, at least irrelevant things. I can only feel my puzzlement and Jōzan's indifference. Perhaps it is in making the attempt to come to terms with that elegant indifference that I, as a child of my own century, have been able to penetrate even a little into the world of that self-consciously elevated, classical beauty that Jōzan chose for himself. Those masks he assumed, those cultural layers he gathered around his persona ultimately allow me to see only what Jōzan felt inclined to reveal and to share. It was only when, over the course of many visits, I became aware that Jōzan did wish to make manifest certain attitudes and accomplishments that *were* important to him that I developed what might be described as a timid and rather peculiar gratitude that he allowed me, through a series of cultural mirrors, to look into what he had identified as the most important elements in his temperament and character. Indeed, it sometimes seems to me that, in spite of the time, distance, and language that separate us, I can locate somewhere in myself a tacit correspondence with his spirit. Yet whatever that connection may be, it comes not from knowledge but from a slowly developing sense of affinity.

II

What, in the modern sense, do we know about Ishikawa Jōzan? Further, are these facts the kind of facts we truly wish to know or need to know? Modern Japanese scholars have attempted to construct a synthetic account of Jōzan's long and eventful life. Written records have been painstakingly pieced together, family registers sifted through, memoirs of his contemporaries combed for relevant details. Though a reasonably complete picture of the man emerges, it gives us at best only shards and slivers of the historical presence. Such bits of information are often fascinating and they do help explain the nature of the cultural background out of which such a man sprang. For those reasons, the facts are worth reciting; indeed, facts and lacunas alike join to form an image.

To a Western reader, Jōzan's dates (1583–1672) reveal nothing special, but in Japan, that span of almost a hundred years is recognized as a period of vast political and cultural change. Jōzan was born into a world in which protracted civil wars consumed the energies of an entire generation. By the time of his death the country was united under the forces of the Tokugawa clan and had entered a long period of isolation, urbanization, and peace.

Jōzan's father and grandfather were well known and respected as brave warriors, men who had long served the cause of the Tokugawas. Jōzan's grandfather died in battle when the boy was scarcely more than a baby, and his father was killed when Jōzan was still a young man of sixteen. Already skilled in the martial arts, he took his career in hand. At a time when military prowess was valued highest, Jōzan appeared to have great prospects, just as his father had predicted. Jōzan participated in the famous battle of Sekigahara in 1600, when Tokugawa Ieyasu (1543–1616) managed to subjugate his rivals and then unite them under his rule. The victorious Ieyasu quickly built a centralized hegemony that developed certain characteristics of a modern nation-state in a relatively short period of time. Jōzan was praised for his nimble actions during the battle; and on one occasion, when he saved the life of a son of Ieyasu, he was publicly feted. It was probably during this period that he developed an interest in Zen Buddhism, as he attended lectures by eminent priests and scholars before favored retainers and family members of the Tokugawa clan.

Little appears to have been recorded concerning Jōzan's personal affairs in the next decade of his life. In 1612, when Jōzan was almost thirty, he was given an opportunity to serve as a personal retainer of one of Ieyasu's sons, an extraordinary honor. Jōzan declined. Few would have refused such access to prestige and power. What was the reason for Jōzan's refusal? This event suggests a shift of vision, and with it the search for a new state of being, that are recognizable as a watershed in Jōzan's life.

Jōzan's inclination to retire could not, however, be immediately followed. Jōzan continued to serve the Tokugawas with considerable recognition for his brave participation in the so-called Summer Campaign of Osaka in 1615, when Ieyasu put down the last rebellious members of Hideyoshi's faction. Jōzan's restlessness remained evident, however. At one point, he left his service briefly, hoping to retire to the great Buddhist temple complex of Myō-shinji in Kyoto. This angered Ieyasu, who placed him under house arrest. Eventually Jōzan was released from the shogun's service. At thirty-three he became a man without a master, a *ronin*. His wish realized, Jōzan retired to Myōshinji, though I have not been able to discover his precise status at the temple.

There were certainly important cultural precedents for Jōzan's action. Perhaps the most celebrated incident was the popular legend of the retirement of Kumagai Naozane (d. 1208), a great Minamoto general in the civil wars of 1185. Forced to kill Atsumori, a young and innocent warrior from the enemy forces, Kumagai renounced the horrors of war in order to do penance as a Buddhist monk. While the historical facts may be at variance with the legend, Kumagai proved a potent cultural symbol known to all as a powerfully tragic figure in literature and the theater. Among literary models, there are even more commanding examples from earlier eras. Saigyō (1118–90), one of the greatest poets in the history of Japanese literature, left his court position at the age of twenty-two to become a wandering monk and occasional recluse. Kamo no Chōmei (1153–1216), from a well-placed family in Kyoto, also retired from society, and in his celebrated diary the *Hōjōki* (A Record of My Hut), he expressed that sense of frailty and transience that is most often associated with the Buddhist literature and thought of the medieval period.

There were other men who, like Jōzan, abandoned their feudal and military duties to find the time to write and think. One of them, Kinoshita Chōshōshi (1569–1649), later became a friend of Jōzan.

In choosing to retire to Myōshinji, Jōzan decided to follow not the path of Buddhism or Japanese poetry but that of Chinese studies. According to written accounts, Jōzan threw himself into a study of the great classical Chinese anthology of literature, the *Wen-hsüan*. Compiled about 530, the *Wen-hsüan* was long a sourcebook for texts on a variety of subjects. Until this period in his life, Jōzan appears to have shown no particular proclivity for literature. Now, with a new opportunity for spiritual development, Jōzan committed himself to the study and the absorption of these great classic texts.

Though this first Kyoto period in Jōzan's life was destined to be a short one, he made a number of famous friends who were to influence his thinking profoundly over the intervening years. One of them was the Confucian scholar Hayashi Razan (1583–1657). Razan was recognized during his lifetime as one of the great scholars of Chinese thought and literature. It is even possible that Jōzan met him earlier, since Razan had become an important figure in the entourage of Ieyasu as early as 1605. Razan introduced Jōzan to the Confucian scholar and philosopher Fujiwara no Seika (1561–1619), perhaps an even more significant figure, who also stirred Jōzan's interests in the Chinese classics. The three often met to discuss literary and philosophical topics.

It is difficult to grasp precisely the effect that the example and the enthusiasms of these men must have had on a man like Jōzan, raised as a Buddhist and imbued with the ethos of a warrior. It is evident from the poems Jōzan has left that he took little interest in the philosophical doctrines propounded by these learned men, but he was very taken with the cultural ideals from China they were attempting to introduce to wider circles in Japan. The idea of a cultivated gentleman living inside and outside society at the same time provided a perfect model for the life that Jōzan had been seeking. He took to these new possibilities with enormous enthusiasm and a dedication that eventually resulted in an ability to compose excellent verse in classical Chinese. Seika, reading one of Jōzan's early efforts, is said to have remarked that "he will surely follow the Way of Poetry." Jōzan's whole persona began to shift.

Ieyasu had encouraged the adoption of Confucian doctrines as a means of organizing and controlling the nation. The cultural and literary ideas that filtered into Japan along with these doctrines brought a whole new sort of artistic and literary self-consciousness and sophistication into Japanese culture. Some of these ideas were brought to Japan by refugees from the Ming dynasty (1368–c. 1644). Well before the fall of the Ming, internal turmoil had caused a number of distinguished Chinese teachers, scholars, and intellectuals to flee to Japan rather than submit to the dictates of a new and foreign regime. The effect on Japanese intellectual life must have been something akin to the enormous change that came to American scientific, intellectual, and artistic life when so many distinguished Europeans, from Einstein and Lévi-Strauss to Hans Hoffmann and Igor Stravinsky, arrived in the United States, fleeing the rise of Nazism. In the Japanese case, men like Razan and Seika, first disciples of some of these eminent Chinese, helped formulate and propagate visions of a new artistic and political order.

Such cosmopolitan attitudes were not altogether new. Indeed, Jōzan was now living in the same city where a shogun of many generations before, Ashikaga Yoshimitsu (1358–1408), had done his utmost as a ruler, politician, and patron of the arts to place Japan in a larger East Asian cultural context.

9

Yoshimitsu loved the Chinese arts, and it is highly appropriate that Jōzan is said to have written the following poem at Kinkakuji, the Golden Pavilion, one of Yoshimitsu's great architectural legacies to the old capital and still one of the great sights of the city. Jōzan was with Fujiwara no Seika and a group of friends viewing the moon.

> Lodging with the monks, we avoid the vulgar dust,
> on a tranquil night look up at autumn sky.
> Winecup in hand, we sit on green moss;
> floating in a boat, pluck *nunawa* plants.
> The Golden Pavilion glitters in the water's depths;
> jade dewdrops moisten the temple fields.
> How lucky that this moon, in a cloudless sky,
> should meet together with us here tonight.[2]

Jōzan admired Seika's life of retreat, in and out of the world at once. His decision to do the same made Jōzan an early prototype of the cultivated gentleman in retirement, the *wen-jen* (Japanese, *bunjin*), often translated as "literati." The cultural attitudes of the literati influenced Japanese culture throughout the Tokugawa period and down to the beginning of this century, when the celebrated modern novelist Natsume Sōseki (1867–1916) still composed classical Chinese verse as a means of personal consolation. The *bunjin* adopted a kind of poetic eclecticism, freely associating forms and ideas in a way that contrasted sharply with the rigidities of official Tokugawa life. While class structure and social behavior were governed by the codes of Chinese neo-Confucianism, literati such as Jōzan chose another Chinese model for inspiration, one that transcended, or stepped aside from, the received pieties. The men who adopted the literati model demonstrated a self-consciousness concerning the purposes and techniques of the various arts they chose to practice. And that self-consciousness makes the painting, poetry, and prose

---

2. The translations of the Chinese poetry of Jōzan quoted in my essay were kindly provided by Jonathan Chaves.

they created surprisingly modern in spirit, once we have grasped their vocabulary.

In spite of his choice, Jōzan was not able to remain immersed in a world of thoughtful pleasure, free of daily duties, for long. He learned within the year that his mother had fallen ill and he was forced to return to work again to support her. Eventually (some scholars think with the aid of Razan) he received a minor post as a retainer of the Asano clan, based in the area of Hiroshima and what now constitutes Wakayama Prefecture, south of Osaka. Jōzan continued in this post, which interested him so little, for twelve years. Nothing is recorded of his life during this long period, while the poet proved the depth of his Confucian filial piety toward his mother. The few poems written in classical Chinese that remain from that time reveal him already spiritually removed from human society. Here is one written in 1628, entitled "Miscellaneous Poem Written While Ill."

> I live at a river bend,
>   the place remote, cut off from dust and dirt.
> Fantastic rocks are planted midst shady trees;
>   an artificial hill begets green moss.
> Beside my pillow—a three-foot sword;
>   outside my window—a single flowering plum.
> Cultivating clumsiness here in this hut of thatch,
>   softly intoning joy, oh how frequent is my joy!

In other works composed during this time, Jōzan referred to the famous verse on chrysanthemums of T'ao Yüan-ming (365–427), the great Chinese poet who retired from the world to become a learned hermit.

> This gentleman of cultivated virtue
> had a hermit's vocation unmatched in his time.
> In service or retirement, he avoided success and failure both;
> he was intelligent, wise and compassionate.
> Caressing a pine tree, he sang the praises of the landscape;
> cane in hand, he inspected the fields.

And the fragrance of his love for a hedgeful of chrysanthemums
has lingered in the air for a thousand years!
With lute and books he drove off his old worries;
poetry and wine helped him forget how poor his family was.
When he became drunk, he finished with Heaven and Earth:
how joyful his body, his shadow, his soul!

Jōzan's mother died in 1635, when the poet was over fifty. He was free. Jōzan immediately left his service with the Asano clan and returned to Kyoto, to his colleague Razan, and to the milieu he had so longed to enjoy. Jōzan went to the temple of Shōkokuji, where he began a lengthy period of reading and study. It must have been a lonely time for him, but a transition from one mental state to another was crucial.

Jōzan was not altogether isolated. He was already widely known as one of the ablest practitioners of Chinese verse in Kyoto. As a result, in 1636 the Tokugawa government asked him to take part in an exchange of verses with the official envoys from Korea, a duty he undertook. On such occasions, the medium of classical Chinese verse served something of the same function that Latin did in medieval Europe, linking cultures with different spoken vernaculars by the written word.

We do not know how Jōzan supported himself in this period. Some have speculated that he continued to receive a small stipend from the Asano family for his years of faithful service, but this cannot be confirmed.

In 1641, at age fifty-eight, Jōzan decided to build the Shisendō, the Hall of Poetry Immortals. He was already an old man for his time.

To construct such a pavilion and garden in mid-seventeenth-century Kyoto was a remarkable gesture. Jōzan purposely removed himself from the society that was being constructed around him and aligned himself with the great Chinese and Japanese recluses whom he most admired. To insist, in those increasingly practical days, that the day-to-day life of a person should be one of the mind and spirit was a powerful ideological statement, and one that could have political overtones as well. Perhaps the most remarkable aspect of the affair was the self-consciousness with which Jōzan accomplished his aims.

In becoming one of the first writers in the Tokugawa period to find beauty in withdrawal, Jōzan used the mentality of the medieval period to breach a hole in the newly erected bulwark of Tokugawa-period thought, setting an example that was to inspire such later figures as the great haiku poet Matsuo Bashō (1644–94), the Buddhist hermit, poet, and calligrapher Ryōkan (1757–1851), and the wandering religious poet Santōka (1882–1940). Jōzan joined a long parade of men who helped define and then extend the limits of their society by adopting alternative and often fanciful modes of thought and behavior that served as models for their contemporaries and posterity.

A suitable setting for withdrawal, meditation, and contemplation had to be created to cultivate such attitudes. Kamo no Chōmei, mentioned above, described the appropriate decor for the retreat of an elegant person who lived in retirement from the world.

On the west, I have built a shelf for holy water, and inside the hut, along the west wall, I have installed an image of Amida. The light of the setting sun shines between its eyebrows. On the doors of the reliquary I have hung pictures of Fugen and Fudō. Above the sliding door that faces north I have built a little shelf on which I keep three or four black leather baskets that contain books of poetry and music and extracts from the sacred writings. Beside them stand a folding koto and a lute.

Along the east I have spread long fern fronds and mats of straw which serve as my bed for the night. I have cut open a window in the eastern wall, and beneath it have made a desk. Near my pillow is a square brazier in which I burn brushwood. To the south of the hut I have staked out a small plot of land which I have enclosed with a rough fence and made into a garden. I grow many species of herbs there.[3]

Yoshida Kenkō (1283–1350), another illustrious predecessor of Jōzan, sug-

---

3. For the full text of the *Hōjōki*, see Donald Keene, ed., *Anthology of Japanese Literature, from the earliest era to the mid-nineteenth century* (New York: Grove Press, 1955), 197–212. The present extract can be found on page 207.

gested the usefulness of similarly simple arrangements in an entry in his
Essays in Idleness.

> A house, I know, is but a temporary abode, but how delightful it is to
> find one that has harmonious proportions and a pleasant atmosphere.
> One feels somehow that even moonlight, when it shines into the quiet
> domicile of a person of taste, is more affecting than elsewhere. A house,
> though it may not be in the current fashion or elaborately decorated, will
> appeal to us by its unassuming beauty—a grove of trees with an inde-
> finably ancient look; a garden where plants, growing of their own ac-
> cord, have a special charm; a verandah and an open-work wooden fence
> of interesting construction; and a few personal effects left carelessly
> lying about, giving the place an air of having been lived in.[4]

Nothing remains of the Kyoto hideaways of Chōmei and Kenkō. Jōzan's
Shisendō, however, can help suggest something of what his predecessors
admired.

I have not been able to locate any useful details as to the manner in which
Jōzan chose his site, nor have I been able to determine what kind of help he
had in planning the gardens and the pavilions. More is known, however, about
Jōzan's remarkable decision to include the portraits of thirty-six Chinese
poets in his central room. Jōzan's reason for choosing thirty-six is not altogether clear, though that number is a significant grouping in the traditional
Chinese psychology of numbers. In Japan, as early as the tenth century, the
highly respected poet Fujiwara no Kintō (966–1041) assembled a famous
anthology, now lost, of thirty-six Japanese poets, suggesting a tradition in
Japan with which Jōzan may have been familiar. In choosing the names of the
thirty-six Chinese poets to be included, a process that consumed half a year
or more, Jōzan consulted with Razan. On the whole, their enthusiasms
matched—with one exception. Razan urged Jōzan to include a portrait of

4. Donald Keene, trans., *Essays in Idleness, the Tsurezuregusa of Kenkō* (New York: Columbia University Press, 1967), 10.

Wang An-shih (1021–86), a noted poet and perhaps the most important Confucian scholar and statesman of his period. Jōzan stubbornly refused; Wang An-shih's character was too suspect to allow his inclusion, no matter how fine his poetry. In this judgment, Jōzan revealed a basic difference between himself and Razan. In the end Wang An-shih's name was dropped from the list of candidates.

Jōzan made no attempt to achieve historical accuracy in the wooden tablets with the portraits of the poets; instead they are iconographic and rather fanciful. Many of these poets were unknown to all but a few scholars of Chinese poetry. The atmosphere they created in the Shisendō must have been quite unusual—at once erudite and detached from the world, rarified and stimulating, marking the hall as a place where unconventional standards were upheld and high-minded virtues practiced. No other poet or writer has ever attempted anything that showed quite such an independence of mind and such daring.

Jōzan in his retirement carried on the traditions of his illustrious literary predecessors, but there were important differences as well. Saigyō, Chōmei, and the others were to a great extent Buddhist recluses who sought to shed the joys and the cares of the mundane world and to seek out a higher level of spiritual truth. Jōzan, on the other hand, had abandoned his Buddhism along with his feudal loyalty when he quit the service of the Tokugawa family. Now, as a professional recluse, living at peace in his self-created and self-sustaining environment, Jōzan set out to explore the world around him. He did so while maintaining a detachment that permitted him to live outside the strict confines of Tokugawa society. Jōzan's poetry seldom reveals the world-weariness or the metaphysical yearning of the writings of his medieval predecessors; rather, he seemed to wish to construct a personal universe in *this* world as an alternative to his society. In his writing, Jōzan used Chinese ideas, aesthetics, and poetic forms to express a range of sentiments that in his view lay beyond the received ideas of his time.

Troubled by illness, poetic powers failing,
youthful idealism—duller with the years.

Lin Pu's dwelling—no horse or carriage tracks;
T'ao Ch'ien's window—outside, the vast universe!
With rare books to read, no unending nights;
this quiet spot is deep within the mountains.
My world is apart from the world of men:
I don't concern myself with their "right" and "wrong."

It is not possible, of course, to know all the books and manuscripts that Jōzan may have admired or read. He certainly knew the history of Chinese poetry as well as any Japanese scholar of his time, and his occasional references to such figures as the legendary ancient mystic philosopher Chuang-tzu and to the writings of the Taoist adept T'ao Hung-ching (456–536) suggest a strong interest in the classical Chinese conceptions of mystic withdrawal.

Living in seclusion, I brush off worldly dust:
remote, secluded, I do not seek neighbors.
Clear-sky moon, this night of austere solitude:
I have no need of someone else to talk to.
Living a hermit in the woods, enjoying nothing to do!
My bramble gate of course is never opened.
Serenely, in perpetual seclusion. . . .
the dog barks, amazed that someone's come to call.

Nevertheless, Jōzan remained in Kyoto and in constant contact with his friends. His withdrawal was mental, perhaps ironic. Jōzan's transfer of intellectual focus away from the older Buddhist conceptions of transience and decay to his present world made him a man of his time. Jōzan may have affected a rejection of society, but he had a fresh and lively interest in the life around him that was, in varying ways, reflected in the writings of most of the great masters of the early Tokugawa period. Ihara Saikaku in fiction and Chikamatsu Monzaemon in the theater both turned to contemporary society for subject matter. Matsuo Bashō, the greatest of the haiku poets, often created poems with a similar frame of reference.

What seems unusual perhaps is that Jōzan chose to express himself in the medium of Chinese verse, or *kanshi,* as it is called in Japanese, rather than in the thirty-one-syllable *waka* or the seventeen-syllable haiku that Bashō was soon to elevate to a form of high art.

The tradition of composing *kanshi* was no longer so strong in Japan at the time Jōzan began to write. His success in the form helped provide *kanshi* with an artistic cachet that restored it as a vital means of expression through to the generation of the novelist Natsume Sōseki, and even beyond.

Writing verse in Chinese had been considered an important skill in the early Heian period, when the Chinese cultural example was particularly powerful. Medieval monks, particularly of the Zen sect, wrote poetry in Chinese, usually referred to as "the poetry of five mountains"—a reference to the five great Zen monasteries in Kyoto and Kamakura. Yet by the time that Tokugawa Ieyasu had begun to suppress the power and prestige of the monasteries, largely for political reasons, the form was no longer a vital one. Jōzan had been introduced to this verse form through the Confucian enthusiasms of his friends, who led him directly to the sources of the great poetry written in previous Chinese dynasties. Jōzan's work, therefore, does not resemble the classical Chinese poetry composed by Japanese predecessors. The breakdown of that earlier tradition in Japan allowed Jōzan a freer range of expression and experiment.

Jōzan may have had contact with another gifted eccentric living in Kyoto, the monk Gensei (1623–88). No records confirming their acquaintance exist, but Gensei was another figure of great importance in the revival of Chinese verse.

Among the various classical Chinese poets known and admired by Jōzan, he had several favorites. His choices, the best of the tradition, may seem unexceptional to modern readers: the recluse Tao Yüan-ming, mentioned earlier, and the two great T'ang poets Tu Fu (712–70) and Li Po (701–62). Tu Fu, of course, was Bashō's revered favorite as well. Jōzan admired the writings of the Ming-dynasty poet Yüan Hung-tao (1568–1610), also a favorite of Gensei.

Jōzan expressed ideas on the functions of poetry. It should not be didactic, but a response to life. It is intensely personal and ultimately it cannot even be discussed with others.

Jōzan lived as a partial recluse at the Shisendō for roughly thirty years. However pleasant his immediate surroundings, though, Jōzan tended to use his pavilion and garden only as a point of repair. He journeyed widely in and around Kyoto, writing poems about a number of sites he enjoyed. Here, for example, is a poem that he wrote when visiting the temple at Ishiyama, a popular spot northeast of Kyoto that commands a fine view of Lake Biwa and long served as a pilgrimage site. Lady Murasaki was supposed to have begun writing her great novel *The Tale of Genji* there.

A Visit to Ishiyamadera

Outside the gates of this monastery
    we tie our little boat,
climb high among the green mists
    and yellow leaves of autumn.
A strip of mountain cloud sweeps off what's left of rain;
a water fall cuts through the cliff,
    plunging hundreds of feet to the lake.
Soaring towers, twisting stone paths—
    truly habitation for immortals!
Fantastic rocks and bizarre escarpments—
    hiding places for spirits!
Here Lady Murasaki wielded her brush
    and wrote *The Tale of Genji*:
was her store of love ever accepted
    as a volume in the Canon?

Here is a poem written at one of Jōzan's favorite sites during the spring season.

Falling Cherry Blossoms at Higashiyama

Filling the ground—cherry blossoms,
    filling the eye—pink clouds;
the blossoms have faded, spring grown old,
    I feel the passing of years.
When the blossoms were at their peak,
    I did not come to visit:
it's not that the blossoms were unfaithful to me;
    I was unfaithful to them.

Although these poems are descriptive, it is clear that they are also constructed to reflect the inner mental and spiritual state of the poet. The poetry is inward looking. Social and political events are not recorded there. Jōzan's poetry, like his calligraphy, served as a means to reflect his growing sense of self-realization.

During his years in Kyoto, Jōzan gained renown as a poet and as a calligrapher. The two, of course, have long been regarded as sister arts in China and Japan, so it is not surprising that Jōzan worked to become highly adept at both. Nor is it remarkable that he introduced, or, more properly, reintroduced, a distinctly Chinese style of calligraphy rather than working in the suppler, more "Japanese" styles widely appreciated at his time. When Jōzan was seventy-one, Emperor Gokōmyō (r. 1643–54) learned of his calligraphic skills and praised Jōzan's artistic abilities. At about the same time, the celebrated painter Kanō Tan'yū (1604–74) created a portrait of Jōzan, which still exists at the Shisendō. Jōzan composed a poem about himself and wrote it on the portrait.

Nyoi in hand, leaning on an armrest,[5]
wearing dark robe and black cap.

---

5. A peculiarly shaped scepter held by Buddhist monks and recluses; the name means "as you like it."

Silent is his noble visage;

brilliant is his spirit.

He communicates with the Creator

and nurtures the Tao within.

A stubborn old man now eighty years old,

a hermit of three-fold Yang.

And who is this hermit, you may ask?

The Mountain Man of the Thirty-Six!

In his old age, Jōzan felt himself very much alone. Seika had died long before; Razan passed away in 1657. In 1663, Jōzan wrote the following.

Inscribed on My Tomb

The old man is eighty—his years are running out!

He gets his coffin ready, a hollow clay jar.

Alone I stand in the midst of this limitless universe;

my body will decompose inside a little hill.

Now increasingly ill, feeling his isolation, Jōzan stayed more and more within his tiny domain, always trying to refuse interviews with the many visitors who continued to seek him out. In a poem reputed to be his last, Jōzan wrote as follows.

Leaning on My Cane

Leaning on my cane within the woods—

shrine trees soaring high all around.

A dog barks at the heels of a beggar;

an ox plows the field, a farmer behind.

My life—the cold stream water;

old, sick—sunset in the sky.

I've known to the full the joys of mist and cloud:

ten years away from a century of life!

Thus ended a life that had begun very differently. The warrior had become a scholar and a poet, the Buddhist had become a Confucian (at least of a free-wheeling sort), and a man raised to cleave to the bonds of personal loyalty to a feudal master had found a life of freedom and detachment.

For us, living in a very different time, this account of Jōzan's life may seem incomplete. How did Jōzan earn his income? What kind of personal and emotional life did he have? Modern Japanese historians, seeking just this kind of information, have offered suggestions about Jozan's sexuality and broached the possibility that he received a portion of his income by acting as a spy for the Tokugawa government. Neither Jōzan nor his original chroniclers discussed or even hinted at such matters—which forces us to examine the relevance of our questions. Answered, or unanswered, they ultimately tell us more about our preoccupations than they do about Jōzan's. After all, in the end, does not the poetry tell us all we truly wish to know? In a remarkable series of passages in his *By Way of Sainte-Beuve,* Marcel Proust wrote that a work of literature

> is the product of a different *self* from the self we manifest in our habits, in our social life, in our vices . . . The implication [for many literary critics] is that there is something more superficial and empty in a writer's authorship, something deeper and more contemplative in his private life . . . In fact, it is the secretion of one's innermost life, written in solitude and for oneself alone, that one gives to the public. What one bestows on private life—in conversation, however refined it may be—is the product of a quite superficial self, not of the innermost self which one can only recover by putting aside the world and the self that frequents the world.[6]

If that is true, then the views Jōzan provides us of his inner life, refracted through the medium of classical Chinese verse, may well come closer to

6. Marcel Proust, *By Way of Sainte-Beuve,* translated by Sylvia Townsend Warner (London: The Hogarth Press, 1984), 76, 79.

revealing the inner truth of the man than any biographical reconstructions. In Jōzan's case, at any rate, I certainly believe it to be so.

III

Even an unpracticed eye can intuit the aesthetic synthesis that binds the visual elements of the Shisendō and its gardens together, however difficult those principles may be to articulate. In the same way, the personality of Jōzan seems fully integrated. Still, we may be led to appreciate him and what he stood for by any number of avenues: poetry, history, art, calligraphy, and philosophy all provide a means to approach him as a totality.

Jōzan fascinates many Japanese because he was one of the first figures in the Tokugawa period to exhibit in his work and life the aesthetic virtue that came to be known as *fūryū,* a term later used in the work of Bashō, who, rather like Jōzan, partially retired from society to become a wanderer searching for aesthetic truth. The term *fūryū* is notoriously difficult to translate. Perhaps a few poems from Bashō's travel diaries can capture the feeling more adequately than a definition.

> The first poetic venture
> I came across—
> The rice-planting songs
> Of the far north.[7]

> To talk casually
> About an iris flower
> Is one of the pleasures
> Of the wandering journey.[8]

---

7. *Bashō, The Narrow Road to the Deep North and Other Travel Sketches,* (Harmondsworth: Penguin Books, 1966), 107.
8. Ibid., 87.

Wild sparrows
In a patch of yellow rape,
Pretending to admire
The flowers.[9]

Fūryū suggests withdrawal from the oversophisticated, ultimately shallow cares of urban life, a pause to search for a natural elegance found in closeness to things at hand and to a simpler, fresher environment.

Those who wrote in the style of *fūryū*, on the other hand, were not literary näifs; Bashō, in particular, like Jōzan, was deeply inspired by his contacts with classical Chinese literature and made use of his enthusiasm and his profound sense of affinities with these sources in his writings. Here, for example, is an extremely famous passage from the writings of the classical Chinese philosopher Chuang Chou (369–286 B.C.), widely known and appreciated in Tokugawa Japan, from his work *Chuang Tzu*.

Once Chang Chou dreamt that he was a butterfly. He did not know that he had ever been anything but a butterfly and was content to hover from flower to flower. Suddenly he woke and found to his astonishment that he was Chuang Chou. But it was hard to be sure whether he was really Chou and had only dreamt that he was a butterfly, or was really a butterfly, and was only dreaming that he was Chou.[10]

Bashō's haiku homage to the Chinese philosopher communicates some of this spirit but in another, perhaps even more playful, mode expressing the *fūryū* mentality.

Arise, arise,
And be my friend,
Dream-butterfly!

9. Ibid., 62.
10. Arthur Waley, trans., *Three Ways of Thought in Ancient China* (New York: Doubleday Anchor Books, 1956), 32.

Jōzan's variation on the same text of Chuang Chou, though written in the form of a classical Chinese lyric, shows a spirit identical to that found in much of Bashō's work; Jōzan shares his understanding of the need for withdrawal and simplicity.

Night Rain—Worrying About the Flowers

I sigh on this rainy late spring night:
the reds and whites that filled the forest are falling to the dust!
Late at night, my soul in dream becomes a butterfly
chasing after each falling petal as it flutters to earth.

The creation of an atmosphere of *fūryū* requires an awareness of the purposes and the limitations of art. It is perhaps this quality that interests me most. Jōzan's consciousness of the ways in which different systems of ideas and aesthetics function allowed him to make deliberate choices. He chose Confucianism over Zen, and from the totality of the Confucian vision he selected an artistic posture rather than a moral stance. These choices were not made blindly or intuitively but openly and consciously, as he sought to make as close a match as possible between his sense of self and the modes of self-expression available. As a good retainer of the Tokugawa, Jozan was expected to subjugate his personal needs to the higher goal of service to his lord. But Jōzan's sense of himself could not be suppressed; and rather than attempt to do so, he chose to remove himself from society. In solitude he assembled a collage of spiritual attitudes to nourish and sustain a style of life that suited his intuitive sense of identity. This quality, it seems to me, makes Jōzan a very modern man, one who might find more sympathy in our century that in his own. While the materials Jōzan put to use as building blocks to assemble his psychological and artistic world—Chinese poetry, calligraphy, a hermitage with its gardens—may be exotic to us, the processes of selection and juxtaposition he used are familiar. In their own ways, Picasso, who used African masks to create new art forms; William Butler Yeats, who borrowed the medieval Japanese Noh play to create a contemporary poetic theater; and even Andy Warhol with his Campbell soup cans, used the same eclectic process. Each artist consciously adopted a "foreign" model and made it his own; the art they created was articulated in a vocabulary that best suited their own temperament, personality, and intellect. Indeed, more often than not it is the personality of the artist alone that can hold these various disparate elements together.

Jōzan enjoyed the challenge of juxtaposing his vision of a Chinese gentleman with that of a Tokugawa samurai to invent a composite image that served as an objectification of the many facets of his personality. In Japan, such a process has wide ramifications. Possession of the self-consciousness and self-understanding required to successfully juxtapose various discrete elements, some at least potentially in conflict, has long been a method at which the Japanese excel. The self-awareness required is by no means limited to artistic endeavor. Within a decade or two of Japan's official opening to the West in 1868, an ability to borrow, to connect, and to juxtapose made the rapid development of public schools, railroads, and a modern army possible as well. Europeans and Americans were astonished at the rapidity with which, by the end of the nineteenth century, the Japanese had successfully adapted their institutions to contemporary world developments—this time amalgamating Western rather than the traditionally employed Chinese conceptions. Japanese entrepreneurs and bureaucrats found it a relatively simple matter to choose from other nations and cultures whatever they felt might serve them in time of rapid change. Plurality of inspiration has long been seen as a virtue in Japanese culture, an attitude which has served it well.

In this regard, Americans in this century, now increasingly committed to plurality ourselves, can sympathize with the process Jōzan chose to create his art and his environment. We do the same thing ourselves, often patching together from disparate sources our lives, our responses, our art, even our politics.

Earlier phases of our own culture—and that of Japan as well—were far less eclectic, far more concentrated on a search for some set of transcendental virtues. Our modern plurality, and Jōzan's, may well seem attractive and familiar but there is the danger that such plurality can signify as well a lack of ultimate commitment, a shallow grounding in the real concerns of civilization. It is important, in the case of Japan, to remember that such poets as Saigyō and Ryōkan were able, by means of their religious convictions, to look far deeper into the human soul than Jōzan ever did.

Accomplishment is ultimately related, of course, to individual talent. Still, the methods chosen also affect the results that can be obtained. Perhaps Jōzan's long search through differing vocabularies of faith and artistic expression precluded scaling the heights. For better or for worse, we in our times are one with him, for we use the same means, searching without lasting commitment. Watching Jōzan assemble then discard one model after another in search of some objective correlative to his evolving self-understanding, we may be equally pleased and startled to discover at work in him a process that we know so well and practice so often in our own day.

Bibliographical Note

I have made use of a number of materials in Japanese to construct the life of Jōzan. By far the most useful account I discovered is a fairly recent one which takes into account a good deal of prior research. The book, by Tadao Narabayashi, is entitled *Bunjin e no Shosha* (Light on the *Bunjin*) and was published by Tankōsha (Kyoto) in 1975. In addition to a lengthy essay on Ishikawa Jōzan, the study deals with two other literati figures of Tokugawa Japan, Tanomura Chikuden (1777–1834), a well-known painter, and Yanagizawa Kien (1706–58), a stylish essayist and translator of Chinese literature.

Jōzan and Poetry

by Jonathan Chaves

When Ishikawa Jōzan commissioned the painter Kanō Tan'yū (1602–74) to produce imaginary portraits of Jōzan's favorite Chinese poets in 1641, the event was a culmination of a thousand years of Japanese fascination with Chinese poetry. Not only did Japanese down through the ages enjoy reading Chinese poetry, but as early as the seventh century they were writing their own *kanshi* (Chinese-language poetry) in the classic *shih* format: four, eight, or more lines with the same number of monosyllabic characters per line—usually five or seven, sometimes four (an archaic meter) or six; rhymes in the even-numbered lines; in some cases parallelism of syntax and imagery in certain couplets; and adherence to elaborate tonal regulations. The difficulty of crafting a merely competent Chinese poem is considerable. For a Japanese, it is particularly challenging because the two languages are linguistically unrelated: classical Chinese is a largely monosyllabic language with uniform (unconjugated) verbs, whereas Japanese is polysyllabic with conjugated verb forms; Chinese word order tends to be subject-verb-object (like English), whereas Japanese has subject-object-verb (like German); and Chinese is one of the rare *tonal* languages of the world (each word must be pronounced with a certain inflection of the voice; these inflections must be taken into consideration when writing poetry), whereas Japanese, like most languages, does not have tones. Finally, Japanese-language poetry does not employ rhyme, whereas Chinese-language poetry does, so that a Japanese poet writing a Chinese poem would not only have to master the very concept of rhyme, but would have to do so in a language with a phonetic structure very different from his own.

And yet by 751, Japanese poetry in Chinese had reached such a degree of quality that the first anthology of such poetry was issued, the *Kaifūsō*, with one hundred thirty poems by sixty-four poets arranged chronologically, the earliest dating from the seventh century. The earliest anthology of Japanese-language poetry, the famous *Manyōshū,* was roughly contemporary with the *Kaifūsō:* the writing of poetry in Chinese goes back to the very beginnings of Japanese literature.

But never before Jōzan built the "Hall of the Poetry Immortals" in 1641 did a single Japanese scholar devote so much of his energy to the study and writing of Chinese poetry. The Shisendō was designed as a shrine to the Chinese poets Jōzan considered most important, thirty-six of them arranged in eighteen pairs. The number thirty-six was inspired by the Thirty-six Immortals of *Waka* (Japanese-language) Poetry, a group familiar through highly stylized imaginary portraits of the poets, with a characteristic poem of each poet inscribed directly beside or above his portrait.

Jōzan carried on lengthy debates with his closest friend, Hayashi Razan (1583–1657), as to which Chinese poets to include. Jōzan initially wanted to include Hsieh T'iao (464–99) of the Chin dynasty, the early-T'ang poets Shen Ch'üan-ch'i (c. 650–713) and Sung Chih-wen (d. 712), and the early-Sung poet Wei Yeh (960–1019). He planned to exclude Han Yü (768–824), a towering figure in the history of Confucian thought but in Jōzan's view not sufficiently distinguished as a poet, and, incredibly, Po Chü-i (772–846)—throughout the centuries the best-loved Chinese poet in Japan, although Jōzan thought him too "coarse" and "vulgar" (in accord, as it happens, with the mainstream Chinese view of Po). Razan succeeded in persuading Jōzan to reverse himself in all these cases. Jōzan stood his ground, however, in barring Tseng Kung (1019–83) and Wang An-shih (1021–86). The debate on Wang—famous not only as a poet but as a prime minister who initiated a series of controversial new economic, political, and military policies—was especially heated, with Razan arguing for the excellence of his poetry and Jōzan expressing contempt for his character. The debate took place in Confucian terms, as might be expected: Jōzan, too, was essentially Confucian in his philosophy, and Razan was the key Confucian adviser to the Tokugawa shoguns; he founded the Yushima Seidō academy for the study of the Confucian classics in 1632. Both men based their arguments on the same passage in the *Analects* (15.22): "The Master said, 'The True Gentleman does not promote a man because of his words; nor does he reject words because of the man.'" Jōzan used the first part of this statement to argue that a

reprehensible character like Wang An-shih ought not to be included merely
because he wrote fine poetry, while Razan used the second part to argue that
one ought not to reject his poetry simply because he was reprehensible. Razan
attempted as well to point out that a number of the immortals of Japanese
poetry were of less than sterling character, but his arguments were to no avail,
and in the end Jōzan insisted on excluding Wang.

The poets chosen by Jōzan are:

1) Su Wu (140?–70 B.C.)
2) Hsieh Ling-yun (385–433)
3) Tu Shen-yen (d. after 705)
4) Li Po (701–62)
5) Wang Wei (701–61)
6) Kao Shih (702?–65)
7) Ch'u Kuang-hsi (fl. 742)
8) Wei Ying-wu (c. 736–c. 792)
9) Han Yü (768–824)
10) Liu Yü-hsi (772–842)
11) Li Ho (791–817)
12) Tu Mu (803–52)
13) Han Shan (early 9th c.)
14) Lin Pu (967–1028)
15) Mei Yao-ch'en (1002–60)
16) Ou-yang Hsiu (1007–72)
17) Huang T'ing-chien (1045–1105)
18) Ch'en Yü-i (1090–1138)

1) T'ao Ch'ien (365–427)
2) Pao Chao (412?–66)
3) Ch'en Tzu-ang (661–702)
4) Tu Fu (712–70)
5) Meng Hao-jan (689–740)
6) Ts'en Shen (715–70)
7) Wang Ch'ang-ling (d. 756)
8) Liu Chang-ch'ing (709–80?)
9) Liu Tsung-yuan (773–819)
10) Po Chü-i (772–846)
11) Lu T'ung (d. 835)
12) Li Shang-yin (813?–58)
13) Ling-ch'e (746–816)
14) Shao Yung (1012–77)
15) Su Shun-ch'in (1008–48)
16) Su Shih (1037–1101)
17) Ch'en Shih-tao (1053–1101)
18) Tseng Chi (1084–1166)

Probably because of his decision to arrange the poets in pairs (an arrangement
more easily discerned in some of the various woodblock editions of the group
than in the current arrangement of the paintings in the Shisendō itself), Jōzan
was compelled to include some rather obscure figures. Ch'u Kuang-hsi, while a
delightful poet, is hardly on a level with the other T'ang masters on the list. Lu
T'ung was a far less important member of the Han Yü circle than, for example,

Chang Chi (c. 776–c. 829)—a poet Jōzan admired and alludes to in his own poems—but Jōzan may have felt that Lu's eccentric style qualified him as a fitting pendant to the "Ghostly Talent," Li Ho. Ling-ch'e, again a good minor poet, was undoubtedly chosen because he was a Buddhist monk; Jōzan needed him to balance the semi-legendary Han Shan ("Cold Mountain"; apparently never ordained a monk but unmistakably a Zen Buddhist poet). By contrast, Shao Yung, although a significant figure in the Neo-Confucian revival, was merely a curiosity as a poet, and is stylistically incompatible with Lin Pu, with whom Jōzan linked him. Wei Yeh, whom Razan persuaded Jōzan to drop, would have been a much better complement to Lin, as both men were noted for their exquisitely observed vignettes of nature in the so-called Late T'ang manner. Tseng Chi is remembered primarily as the teacher of the great Lu Yu (1125–1210), whose poetry Jōzan knew and admired, but Lu himself is not included. Indeed, the strangest feature of the group is that it ends in the late Northern to early Southern Sung, and it excludes all of the great Southern Sung masters, such as Lu Yu. Did Jōzan simply run out of numbers, and could he not bear to drop any of the earlier figures to make room for Lu? Or did he feel obligated on the grounds of theory to deemphasize later poets? As we shall see, Jōzan admired Sung poetry but upheld the primacy of the T'ang.

Jōzan seems to have enjoyed ready access to books of Chinese poetry, including recent or even contemporary works of the late Ming. He maintained a close friendship with Ch'en Yuan-yun (1587–1671), a Chinese emigré who introduced to Japan the works of the leader of the Kung-an "Individualist" school in late Ming letters, Yuan Hung-tao (1568–1610). Ch'en was also a painter and a master of the Chinese martial art of *kung-fu*. He and other Chinese emigrés brought books from China to Japan, as did the Chinese merchants who were making regular trips to Nagasaki during this period. In one of his letters, Jōzan speaks in glowing terms of the "literary collection(s)" of Ts'ao Hsueh-ch'üan (1574–1646). Ts'ao was a Ming-loyalist suicide whose *Shih-ts'ang Li-tai Shih-hsuan* (An Anthology of Poetry Down Through the Ages from the Stone Granary—"Stone Granary" was a studio-name of Ts'ao's), printed in 1632 in five hundred six chapters (*chüan*), was possibly the most comprehensive compendium of Chinese poetry that had been compiled to date. If this is the work Jōzan refers to in his letter (it is also possible that he had merely seen the collected writings of Ts'ao), he had access through it to a truly representative sampling of the entire corpus of Chinese poetry.

Jōzan's long life spanned the late Ming to early Ch'ing dynasties, a time of traumatic change and philosophical and religious questioning for the Chinese, as in 1644 the Ming dynasty fell not to native Chinese but rather to the nomadic Manchus. The disturbing parallel with the earlier fall of the Sung dynasty to the invading Mongols in 1279 led to searching debates about the reasons for the loss to foreigners of the "Heavenly Mandate" to rule China. The literary scene during this period was a complex one; Chinese scholars contemporaneous with Jōzan, such as Ch'ien Ch'ien-i (1582–1664), were attempting to come to terms with the disagreements between the so-called "Former Seven and Latter Seven Masters" and the Kung-an school under Yuan Hung-tao. In general, the fourteen "orthodox masters" called for prose to emulate that of the great Chinese historian, Ssu-ma Ch'ien (c. 145–c. 85 B.C.), while poetry, in their view, could never rise beyond the level achieved during the golden age of the High T'ang, and for them the High T'ang-poet Tu Fu represented the zenith of poetic excellence. An aspiring poet ought to strive to emulate his style, not because of some arbitrarily admired quality it might possess but rather because through it, in the view of this Archaist school of thought, it was possible to penetrate to fundamental underlying principles of composition believed to be innate in the natural order of things. In other words, Tu Fu's greatness lay not in his personal style but in his ability to transcend the merely personal and arrive at natural principles. Yuan Hung-tao, by contrast, while admiring Tu Fu, felt that the individual poet must express his personal innate sensibility (*hsing-ling*). Ch'ien Ch'ien-i accepted the concept of expression of sensibility, while decrying what he considered to be the excesses to which certain Kung-an followers went; he rejected the rigidity of the orthodox masters even as he agreed with them in admiring Tu Fu and, through Tu Fu, fine poetic craftsmanship. Ch'ien Ch'ien-i attempted to forge a synthesis of the strongest points of both camps— the expressiveness of the Individualists, and the craftsmanship of the Archaists.

Jōzan occupies a position remarkably similar to that of Ch'ien Ch'ien-i, subscribing to elements of both the orthodox Archaist theory (and praising some of the writings of the orthodox masters), and the Individualist theory of Yuan Hung-tao, especially "innate sensibility" and Yuan's opposition to over-emphasis on imitation of past models. In addition, Jōzan's appreciation of Sung-dynasty poetry (and his quite extensive knowledge of it) is in harmony with a reawakening of interest in the Sung poets in the late Ming to early Ch'ing, championed originally by the Individualists, partially to counter what they saw as too great a stress by the Archaist school on the High T'ang. The close convergence of views between Jōzan and Ch'ien Ch'ien-i, a leading arbiter of Chinese taste, might demonstrate the care with which Jōzan followed intellectual currents in China, but when it is noted that the first major collection of Ch'ien's writings, the *Ch'u-hsueh Chi,* was printed in 1643, while the Shisendō was built in 1641, we must wonder whether Jōzan was not in fact anticipating certain developments in China, or at least thinking along paral-lel lines.

Jōzan's knowledge of Chinese poetry allowed him to recreate the lifestyle of a Chinese scholar-recluse like T'ao Ch'ien or Lin Pu. At the same time, it had a public aspect: the exchange of Chinese-language poetry played a role in contemporary diplomacy throughout East Asia, and the ability to read, write, and discuss that poetry intelligently served as a *lingua franca.* In 1637, Jōzan met with a Korean delegation to Japan, and exchanged poems and views on poetry with a certain Korean "professor" of *kanshi* and perhaps with others in the entourage as well. Like the Japanese, Koreans had for centuries written verse in Chinese in addition to their own superb Korean-language poetry. In the exchange between Jōzan and the Korean visitor, a partial transcription of which survives in Jōzan's works, the Korean professor praises Jōzan as the Li Po and Tu Fu of Japan, expressing the Archaist view that T'ang poetry is best, and Sung and Yüan poetry of little value. Despite the warmth of this meeting, Jōzan, in a letter to Razan's third son, Hayashi Shunsai (1618–80), criticizes the poetry of a Korean visitor (this same professor?) for being shallow and vulgar because he only admires the Po Chü-i manner.

Jōzan's own poetry is of very high quality. Burton Watson, the leading Western expert on *kanshi,* reports that in a history of Japanese *kanshi* Emura Hokkai (1713–88) names Jōzan and the monk Gensei (1623–68) as the two best *kanshi* poets of their time. Jōzan's poetry has an unmistakable Sung flavor, with its understated, relatively straightforward diction (partially derived from the very Po Chü-i about whom Jōzan, ironically, had mixed feelings), and subject matter drawn from ordinary life. While more mechanical *kanshi* practitioners later produced innumerable poems about places in China they would never see, Jōzan set poem after poem in places he knew and had visited: Mount Fuji (page 35); Kinkakuji (Temple of the Gold Pavilion, page 35); Higashiyama (the Eastern Mountains) in Kyoto (page 40); and especially, of course, his beloved Shisendō garden. It is in the Shisendō poetry—some of the best garden poetry in the *kanshi* genre—that Jōzan strikes his distinctive keynote of tranquility. Although Jōzan is learned in Chinese literature and frequently alludes to Chinese classics and poets, he invokes masterpieces of Japanese literature as well—the episode of Atsumori's death from the *Tale of the Heike* (page 36), for example, and *The Tale of Genji* (page 41). In poems that make use of Japanese personal names or place names, Jōzan often faced the problem of using characters which ordinarily have polysyllabic readings in Japanese as monosyllables—that is, he had to substitute the Chinese-derived *on* reading for the indigenous *kun* reading. For example, in "A Visit to Ishiyamadera," (page 41) the penultimate line reads in Chinese, *tzu shih hui hao chi yuan shih.* In the Japanese *on* reading it is *shi shi ki go ki gen ji,* or "[Here] Lady Murasaki wielded [her] brush [and] wrote [*The Tale of*] *Genji.*" The last two characters together are ordinarily read "Genji" in the *on* reading and so they fit right in (one syllable each); but the first character, when used as the name of the author of the great novel, is read in *kun* pronunciation with no less than four syllables—Murasaki. Jōzan fit the character quite neatly to the seven-character meter, compelling the reader to adopt the *on* reading *shi.*

The Sung-derived realism of Jōzan's poetry is particularly clear in his choice of imagery—*bentō* (lunches in stacked lacquer boxes), portable braziers and lamps for picnics, and other familiar objects of Japanese life appear (see page 40). Poems are devoted to native Japanese birds (page 39) or even a type of mosquito (page 51), this last poem title reminiscent of a poem on the movements of a fly by the Sung poet Yang Wan-li (1127–1206). Although the idea of Chinese-language poems by a Japanese poet might appear somewhat artificial at first, the world created by Jōzan in his *kanshi* poems is vibrantly real and rings true as a portrait of his Japan.

Was Jōzan's great love for Chinese poetry and culture in any way reciprocated? That is, was his *kanshi* poetry known and read in China? As far as I can tell, Jōzan's poetry—and indeed Japanese *kanshi* in general, exclusive of isolated diplomatic exchanges—was not introduced to the Chinese until 1882, when the great Ch'ing-dynasty scholar, Yü Yueh (1821–1907) was asked by the Japanese journalist, Kishida Ginji (1833–1905) to produce an anthology of Japanese *kanshi* poetry from materials that Kishida presented to him, including poems by both Jōzan and Hayashi Razan. At first, Yü Yueh was reluctant to undertake the project, but finally decided to do so, and in 1883 he completed the *Tung-ying Shih-hsuan* (An Anthology of Poems from the Eastern Isles-of-Paradise) in forty-four chapters, consisting of selections from over five hundred poets, including Jōzan. According to Yü, this work was printed and circulated in Japan (it is unclear whether copies were ever available in China), so the goal appears to have been not to introduce Japanese *kanshi* to a Chinese readership, but rather to provide Japanese aficionados with the pleasure of discovering how a leading Chinese scholar would pick and choose among the best of native *kanshi* poets.

Yü did write a short, two-chapter work entitled *Tung-ying Shih-chi* (A Record of Poetry from the Eastern Isles-of-Paradise), also in 1883, which was later (1889) included in his complete writings and achieved a wide circulation in China. In this book, Yü selected one hundred fifty Japanese poets from the over five hundred he had anthologized and provided short biographies of them with critical appreciations of their work and selected lines. The first poet treated in this book is Hayashi Razan; the fourth, Jōzan. Employing one of the rich but sometimes ambiguous two-character expressions preferred by Chinese critics of poetry (and also of calligraphy and painting), Yü describes Jōzan's poetry as *p'u-mao*—frank (or honest) and full of feeling. He quotes Jōzan's couplet,

> Years [of] youth: three-foot sword;
> realm [of] old-age: single bamboo cane

and comments, "These ten words suffice to convey this old man's entire life."

A Selection of Poems
by Ishikawa Jōzan

Mount Fuji

1.
Immortals travel to this peak beyond the clouds;
    a dragon hibernates in the waters of its caves.
Snow like white silk,
    rising mist like a handle:
this white fan hangs upside down
    in the sky of the eastern seaboard.
2.
All year around, the snow has stayed white,
    for several thousands of autumns;
on every side, dark coldness
    touches tens of provinces.
Looking up at the layered peak,
    it seems to be carved out:
among the clouds, a huge *manju*-dumping
    stuffed all full of earth.

On the night of the fourteenth day of the eighth month of the year *kigai* of the Genna period (September 8, 1623) I viewed the moon at the Kinkakuji together with Tameharu and Kyuen.

Lodging with the monks, we avoid the vulgar dust,
on a tranquil night look up at autumn sky.
Winecup in hand, we sit on green moss;
floating in a boat, pluck *nunawa* plants.
The Golden Pavilion glitters in the water's depths;
jade dewdrops moisten the temple fields.
How lucky that this moon, in a cloudless sky,
should meet together with us here tonight.

Poet's note: At the time the first *nunawa* had just appeared in the lake.

Chrysanthemums in a Vase

These frosty branches and dew-laden leaves
　　have left the dusty garden
and moved up to this alcove
　　where they put forth lustrous bloom.
The flowers recognize Master T'ao
　　and do not change expression:
here, in their vase, the Chin dynasty
　　goes on in a world of its own.

Master T'ao refers to T'ao Ch'ien (also T'ao Yüan-ming, 365–427), one of China's greatest
poets, included by Jōzan among the thirty-six immortals of poetry. T'ao, who lived during the
Chin dynasty, was famous among other things for his love of chrysanthemums, and for this
reason nearly every poem or painting on these flowers alludes in some manner to him or to his
own poems on the subject. Here, Jōzan presents himself as a modern-day T'ao Ch'ien.

The Tomb of Atsumori

Four hundred years ago there was a youth
so handsome with his lovely hair and brow!
He went to battle, bow and sword in hand,
attended court, playing flutes and strings.
On the sand, a horseman came riding, holding a war fan high;
from the sea, the youth looked back while galloping to the ship. . . .
If he had played a barbarian tune on his flute, "Greenleaf,"
surely the enemy would have opened rank and allowed him to retreat!

For the famous story of Atsumori as told in the *Tale of the Heike (Heike Monogatari)*, see Donald
Keene, ed., *Anthology of Japanese Literature* (1955), 179–81. Such details as the war fan held
aloft by Atsumori's pursuer, Kumagai, as well as the flute discovered by Kumagai on the body
of the slain Atsumori are drawn from this account.

From a Boat at Night, Gazing at the Kannon Hall

Below the cliff, riding in a boat,
　　I think of climbing up—
the mountain temple is silent, it seems
　　to have no monks.
A falling star—a single dot—
　　plunges into the waves:
it is a beam of lamplight
　　from the Kannon Hall above.

Murotsu

High on the mountains—shrines of the gods;
   below the mountains—springs.
Along the river, following the bank,
   houses strung together.
Ancient pine trees twist and lean,
   overhanging cliffs;
frosty leaves come floating down
   beside the waterfront.
Out of windows hang fishing lines—
   so many anglers here!
To banisters are tied the hawsers
   of boats that come and go.
Now a bell reverberates throughout this distant village:
it is sunset; the fishermen haul in their nets
   and come back into port.

In the Boat—Feelings

I sit in a daze at my cabin window—
   I've lost track of the time:
watching mountains, watching water—
   unable to fall asleep!
This body of mine has floated along,
   over rivers, over lakes. . . .
I feel ashamed when the sand gulls
   stare at me with cold eyes.

Gardening Chrysanthemums, I Think of Yüan-ming

This gentleman of cultivated virtue
had a hermit's vocation unmatched in his time.
In service or retirement, he avoided success and failure both;
he was intelligent, wise and compassionate.
Caressing a pine tree, he sang the praises of the landscape;
cane in hand, he inspected the fields.
And the fragrance of his love for a hedgeful of chrysanthemums
has lingered in the air for a thousand years!

With lute and books he drove off his old worries;
poetry and wine helped him forget how poor his family was.
When he became drunk, he finished with Heaven and Earth:
how joyful his body, his shadow, his soul!

For T'ao Ch'ien (Yüan-ming), see the note to the poem *Chrysanthemums in a Vase*. The fourth couplet of the present poem alludes to T'ao's most famous use of the chrysanthemum image, the fifth line of the fifth poem in his great sequence, *Drinking Wine:* "I pluck chrysanthemums beneath the eastern hedge." Jōzan chose the poem in question to represent T'ao in the poetry immortal paintings. The last line here also alludes to a well-known work of T'ao's, a group of three related poems in which T'ao presents a three-way debate among his body, shadow, and soul.

Thanking Someone for Making Me a Gift of a Melon

On its jade skin the dew has not dried:
a melon worthy of the Imperial Carver's knife!
It can dispel the heat of summer,
the green ice chilly as it touches your teeth.

In my garden there is an apricot tree which flowers but does not bear fruit. I have written this quatrain to request the tree to bear both flowers and fruit. (Recently this tree did put forth fruit for the first time, thousands of them! When my neighbors saw this, they exclaimed, "Was this Heaven's will, or simply something which happened naturally with the passage of the seasons?")

In the beginning, in the grove of Tung Feng,
    each piece of fruit helped cure an impoverished patient.
Your many blossoms would lead one to expect
    that you should have fruit as well,
but year after year—nothing at all,
    a waste of the breezes of spring.

Tung Feng was a legendary physician of the Three Kingdoms period in China (third century A.D.) who gave apricots to people as medicine in exchange for grain. He had a grove of his own apricot trees.

Making Fun of the "Nightingale" of My District
For Not Being the True Nightingale

In spring you may perch on the tips of bamboo and sing quite beautifully,
but your body, your features—even your voice are different from the nightingale's!
In appearance you seem a relative of the *misosazai* wren:
how fortunate you are that people call you a "nightingale."

Jōzan is referring to the *uguisu*, the Japanese bush warbler, beloved for its song and sometimes referred to in poetry as the nightingale, or *ying*, a Chinese bird fabled in legend and poetry.

Spring Morning—Orally Improvised

White and fragrant, white and fragrant,
    plums put forth their bloom;
burgeoning green, burgeoning green,
    sprouts of grass appear.
Flying, flying, one by one,
    warblers flit through willows;
fluttering, floating, fluttering, floating,
    butterflies search for flowers.
Soft and gentle, soft and gentle,
    wind disturbs the dew;
vague and misty, vague and misty,
    fog merges with the clouds.
Distant, distant, at the horizon,
    eastern sky turns bright;
dazzling, glowing, dazzling, glowing,
    rises the blossom of the sun.

Dog Island

Lost in mist, the island floats on water;
on it appears the vague form of a beast.
When did this Tengu fall from Heaven and turn into a stone?
It crouches there as if barking at river travelers.

The Tengu ("Heavenly Dog") is a complex creature in Chinese and Japanese mythology. According to various accounts, it can be a star or comet, a form of badger, or a frankly mythical animal with a human body, long nose, and wings.

Hell Valley
—at Arima Hot Springs

Beyond the village, this no man's land—
people call it the Avici Hell.
At sundown, woodcutters tremble with fear;
clouds gather, angry thunder roars.
Mountain spirits weep tears of dark rain,
apes of the night howl at the moon.
In the loneliness of this desolate valley
the soul snaps at the nighjar's cry!

Avici Hell is the Hell of Ceaseless Suffering in Buddhist eschatology and the worst of the various hells to which the deceased can be consigned.

On All Souls' Festival,
Visiting the White Cloud Pavilion of Seiken
to View the Torches on the Mountains

At dusk in brilliant glory the festive lights are lit,
guiding the returning souls around the capital.
Thousands of torches burn along the mountain roads:
amazed we see golden dragons leaping to the sky!

Noma Seiken (1608–76) was a disciple of Jozan's closest friend, Hayashi Razan. The fifteenth day of the seventh month of the lunar calendar marked the Buddhist Avalamba (All Souls') Festival, during which services were held to release the souls of the dead from purgatory and guide them to earth where they would be provided with food.

Spring Scene in the Eastern Mountains

People who go to Higashiyama ("Eastern Mountains") often stay until late at night. Therefore, even though it may be daylight when they depart, they bring portable lamps along with them.

Higashiyama in the third month—the place for cherry blossoms!
private curtains, mats to sit on cover the old graves.
And the servants—back and forth—what is it they bring?
Braziers, *bentō* meals, and also portable lamps.

A Visit to Ishiyamadera

Outside the gates of this monastery
    we tie our little boat,
climb high among the green mists
    and yellow leaves of autumn.
A strip of mountain cloud sweeps off what's left of rain;
a waterfall cuts through the cliff,
    plunging hundreds of feet to the lake.
Soaring towers, twisting stone paths—
    truly habitation for immortals!
Fantastic rocks and bizarre escarpments—
    hiding places for spirits!
Here Lady Murasaki wielded her brush
    and wrote *The Tale of Genji*:
was her story of love ever accepted
    as a volume in the Canon?

Ishiyamadera (Stone Mountain Temple) is located near Otsu on Lake Biwa. Today a statue of Lady Murasaki depicts her in the process of writing her masterpiece, *The Tale of Genji*, in one of the chambers of the temple.

Delighted at the Completion of the Portraits of the Poetry Immortals

I spend old age among mountains and streams
    at the Temple of the One Vehicle,
body at rest, mind at peace,
    far from the hustle and bustle.
Now the portraits of the Poetry Immortals
    have been hung up in their hall:
elegant, refined, again there are pictures
    done in trompe-l'oeil style!

The great Chinese painter, Chang Seng-yu (active 500–550) was said to have originated the trompe-l'oeil style, in which the pictures appeared to be three dimensional from a distance, at the Temple of the One Vehicle in China, from which the temple near Shisendō apparently took its name.

In the second month of summer of the year *teigai* (1647), together with some friends, I traveled by boat from Otsu to see the fireflies at Yashima.

> The rain has stopped—the calm lake feels
>   like autumn in mid-summer;
> evening—we watch the boats
>   move past reed-grown islets.
> A skyful of stars turns above the bank—
> tens of thousands of brilliant pearls
>   scattered in evening waters!
> Cold flames leap in the void
>   like torches held aloft;
> flying lights brush the water's surface;
>   we fear our boat has caught fire!
> Night seems like day among the mountains and streams:
> a shame that the Sui dynasty's Emperor Yang
>   can't come here for a visit.

The Great Man

Two nights ago, I dreamed of the line, "Beyond the realm of phenomena, there is a Great Man." I have developed this into a full poem of eight couplets. While not aspiring to an imitation of Ssu-ma Hsiang-ju's prose poem, in the leisure time I have while recuperating from an illness, this will serve to express what is in my heart.

> Beyond the realm of phenomena, there is a Great Man
> who controls everything within the universe.
> With one gesture he uproots the mountains,
> with a few steps covers ten thousand miles.
> K'ua-fu is no match for him;
> he wouldn't give Kung-kung a glance!
> Opening his shirt, he sits on the K'un-lun Mountains;
> raising his robe, he fords the River Jo!
> The bands of cloud in a clear sky are his clothes drying out;
> the sacred Mount T'ai is his armrest.
> When he's angry, the thunder rumbles;
> when he blows, the plants and trees wither away.

Compared to him, P'an-ku is a mayfly
and Dragon Earl is nothing but an ant.
He wanders freely at the Gate of the Mysterious Female;
riding on the Void, he will never die.

Ssu-ma Hsiang-ju (179–117 B.C.) was a great court poet of the Han dynasty, famous for his lengthy and highly ornate prose poems (*fu*). One of these, to which Jōzan alludes, was known as the *Ta-jen fu, Prose Poem on the Great Man*. K'ua-fu, Kung-kung, and P'an-ku are various mythological heroes of antiquity in China. P'an-ku was believed to have been the creator of the universe. The K'un-lun Mountains and River Jo are locations in Chinese mythology. The K'un-lun Mountains are sometimes said to represent the Himalayas. The Mysterious Female is one of the epithets used for the Tao in the *Tao Te Ching*.

Falling Cherry Blossoms at Higashiyama

Filling the ground—cherry blossoms,
    filling the eyes—pink clouds;
the blossoms have faded, spring grown old,
    I feel the passing of years.
When the blossoms were at their peak,
    I did not come to visit:
it's not that the blossoms are unfaithful to me;
    I was unfaithful to them.

Singing My Feelings

In this house, a craze for calligraphy and poems;
outside the gate, no tracks of horse or carriage.
Enjoying tea, I remember Ou-yang Hsiu, the scholar;
viewing flowers, think of poet Chang Chi.
Insects' wings strike against the paper window;
cat's claws scratch at the straw mat.
My plan was simple—retire early.
To this day I've had peace of mind.

Ou-yang Hsiu (1007–72) was a Sung-dynasty scholar of great refinement and an outstanding poet. He was included by Jōzan among the Thirty-six Poetry Immortals. Chang Chi (c. 776–c. 829) was an important T'ang poet, one of the best to be excluded from the Poetry Immortals by Jōzan.

Indulging in Laziness

Hidden, remote, I decline all visitors;
holding to simplicity, I emulate Yüan-ming.
At night I dislike the weight of heavy blankets;
walking I keep the bamboo cane's lightness in hand.
The sky has cleared—a mountain village shows;
the wind has stopped—evening slopes descend.
My Way is modeled on the Primal Transformation;
I have no desire to live hundreds of years.

Yüan-ming refers to T'ao Ch'ien (365–427), the famous recluse and one of the Poetry Immortals.

Feelings on a Summer Day

My house is not a place where you suffer from the heat:
fresh shade sprinkled by a waterfall!
At the foot of the wall, a rabbit crouches;
from the eaves a bat hangs at its ease.
In hidden wanderings, I lack Ch'iu Chung as companion;
tranquil, at peace, even more than Ch'eng-hsien.
I move my bed out beside the pond:
morning after morning, how I love the white lotus!

Ch'iu Chung was one of the few visitors allowed by Chiang Hsu, the famed hermit of the Han dynasty. No one by the name Ch'eng-hsien seems to fit the context of Jōzan's line; presumably he had in mind a retired scholar or recluse.

Lamenting My Old Age

I grow old—the horse of time
    is a thoroughbred!
My body and soul are still together
    but it isn't the old me.
Forty-three years have passed away
    like a bolt of lightning:
of my old friends, not one man still remains.

Poet's note: This refers to the period of time since the Osaka Rebellion. This poem was written in 1657. The poet was seventy-four years old at the time.

Expressing Emotions

1.

Troubled by illness, poetic powers failing,
youthful idealism—duller with the years.
Lin Pu's dwelling—no horse or carriage tracks;
T'ao Ch'ien's window—outside, the vast universe!
With rare books to read, no unending nights;
this quiet spot is deep within the mountains.
My world is apart from the world of men:
I don't concern myself with their "right" and "wrong."

2.

A thatch-roofed house of three rooms,
the garden with the spirit of antiquity.
Living in retirement, removing bookworms from books,
climbing the mountains for views which lighten my heart.
The rain stops, snails retreat into their shells;
the well-water is pure, reflecting bamboo leaves.
There's not a single thing I must do in my life:
as I get older, the Tao takes firmer root.

3.

For years, I've been companion to the deer;
I've never been happy to hear visitors' footsteps.
If guests appear, they sully my paths;
when birds have flown away, the garden is truly peaceful.
I cut my own patch of moss, like Kuan Ning's mat;
the pine trees sing the tunes of Tai K'uei's lute.
My real friends—all of them are in the grave,
are as far from me as the Shen star from the Shang.

Lin Pu (967–1028) and T'ao Ch'ien (365–427), two famous recluse-poets of the Sung and Chin dynasties respectively, were both included by Jōzan among the Poetry Immortals. Kuan Ning (158–241), although the descendant of great officials, found himself caught up in the chaotic events of the end of the Han dynasty and experienced great poverty. He maintained an austerely aloof attitude toward men of power. When a friend of his who was sitting with him on the same mat rose to greet a wealthy official, Kuan cut his section of matting away from that of his friend, saying, "You are no friend of mine." Tai K'uei (d. 396) was a great *ch'in* (zither) master.

Singing of Flowers

Flowers, flowers, innumerable flowers!
Flowers fade then flowers bloom again.
Flowers seem to vie with flowers:
red flowers dazzling among brilliant white flowers!

Leisurely Wanderings

I dust off a place by the window to sit and read,
or stand in the garden and watch the animals and plants.
The water has gone down—the fish are restless;
the rain has stopped—cicadas chant in the mountains.
A waterfall from the cliff sprays away the heat;
my sandals and cane help me as I walk.
Forever I have wakened from the dream within a dream;
alone I wander through this world beyond the world.
How could I accept the gift of T'ien Tzu-fang?
I presume to admire the verse of "Overturned Cart."
I'll just go on indulging in laziness,
my life like an empty boat, not anchored or moored.

Tzu-ssu, grandson of Confucius, while living in great poverty was once offered a coat of white fox fur by a certain T'ien Tzu-fang. Tzu-ssu refused to accept it. "Overturned Cart" refers to a poem by Shih Su (late twelfth century) with the lines, "Body like an overturned cart—totally useless; / mind like a bright mirror without a speck of dust." Inspired by this couplet, a Buddhist monk dubbed himself Overturned Cart and wrote, "The wrecked cart actually *does* have a use: / it serves to cut off the myriad thoughts and schemes."

Recording My Feelings

Years ago I went into retirement
and built this place beside the mountain.
Among the trees there is no worldly noise;
beneath the eaves, the tranquil flow of a stream.
Once I sought the benefit of books;
now I'm more at home playing with sand.
And after all, what isn't a child's game?
Confucius and Lao Tzu—each is a cupful of earth.

Poet's note to line six: This is a child's game.

Impromptu Feelings

Lazy, living at a time of peace,
I've roosted for years in this wooded place.
Life and death I leave to Heaven and Earth;
withdrawal and service?—lethargic as a cow!
My body hidden away, I decline all visitors;
my spirit turned inward, nourish old age and poverty.
Of ten poems I write, eight or nine are clumsy—
I go by feeling and don't seek perfect form.

Eyeglasses

The eyeglasses add vision to my eyes—
such clarity and joy in old age!
In reading now, I put Li Chu to shame;
in "observing phenomena" I've replaced Shao Yung.
I wield my brush and write characters the size of fly-heads;
I could easily shoot a bug off the eyelash of a mosquito.
A marvelous way to get rid of foggy vision—
Is this not a technique for returning to youth?

Li Chu was a man with legendary powers of vision. He is often represented by statues in Chinese temples. Shao Yung (1012–77) was a major Neo-Confucian philosopher of the Sung dynasty and an eccentric poet. One of his works is entitled *On the Observation of Phenomena*. (It is assumed here that the character *na* in Jōzan's fourth line as printed is a misprint for Shao.) Jōzan included Shao Yung among the Poetry Immortals, even though his reputation as a poet in China was never particularly high. In line six, Jōzan has conflated two allusions to the Taoist classic *Lieh Tzu*. A man named Chi Ch'ang perfected his archery to the point where he could shoot a flea hanging from a thread without breaking the thread. The "bug" (*chiao-ming*) in the poem is an insect so tiny that it swarms and gathers on the eyelashes of mosquitoes without the mosquitoes noticing.

In the Garden—Improvised

The year's second month, living in the mountains—
embroidered cherry blossoms beautiful to view!
I am so moved, dinner is forgotten—
old, I mourn spring's passing more than ever.
Swift sounds of wind through a thousand blossoms;
setting sunlight halfway down the bamboo.
This poem is done—I'm too lazy to revise it;
I'll leave every word as it came from my brush.

Impromptu

A long dipper to water the flowers,
a little knife to cut open the melon;
for coolness I open the northern window,
then lean on the pillow and read *Chuang Tzu*.
Towards sunset, crows caw raucously;
a slight breeze wafts the lights of fireflies.
Done with chanting poems, I re-read my old work:
there's no denying it has many flaws.

Summoned by Master Takeda I went to Ichihara. On the way I was
disturbed by the signs of a disastrous year. (From the first month of spring
through the third month, there were fires at Takeshiro. From the first month
of autumn through the tenth month it rained heavily in the Kyoto area.)

Why was this a year of such disaster?
Beggars cry out along the roads.
Autumn downpours fell four months straight;
wind-swept fires raged all three months of spring.
Woodcutters can find no firewood;
farmers have given up their crops.
In the capital, rice sells for thousands:
how can the poor get anything to eat?

In the lunar calendar, the first three months of the year are the spring, the following three
(months four, five, six) the summer, the following three the autumn (months seven, eight, nine)
and the final three the winter (months ten, eleven, twelve). Hence the "autumn rains" referred
to in the title and in line three of the poem lasted all autumn and continued through the first
month of winter.

An Autumn Night: Depicting Activity Within Quiescence

White hairs in autumn—I am moved by the scene.
In the mountains I live, companion to the moon, passing what's left of my life.
Late at night, the ten thousand sounds of nature have all given way to silence—
I can only hear the sound of the water mortar knocking against the rock.

The "water mortar" was the bamboo tube set up by Jōzan in his garden in such a manner
that it would periodically fill with water and then empty out, falling to a rock below with a
sonorous echo.

Night Rain—Worrying About the Flowers

I sigh on this rainy late spring night:
the reds and whites that filled the forest are falling to the dust!
Late at night, my soul in dream becomes a butterfly,
chasing after each falling petal as it flutters to the earth.

Inscribed on My Tomb

The old man is eighty—his years are running out!
He gets his coffin ready, a hollow clay jar.
Alone I stand in the midst of this limitless universe;
my body will decompose inside a little hill.

Chanting Poems While Ill

In old age I don't consult doctors—
life and death both suit me just fine!
Lamplight shadows flicker on the tattered bedscreen;
from my sickbed I listen to the water clock's slow drip.
My teeth are all loose—food has lost its flavor;
my body, so thin—I get callouses when I sit.
This poem is done, I'm too lazy to write it down:
I'll chant it out loud and have the boy do the work.

The Year Jin'in (1662), Summer, the Fifth Month— A Poem on the Earthquake

I hear that when the great earthquake
    struck the capital
the crowds panicked, people were running around
    in the streets.
Mountains crumbled, the earth cracked,
    rivers seemed to stand on end!
Only the birds, flying through the air,
    had no idea what was going on.

Expressing My Feelings

The mountain village has plenty of vegetables—
I may be old and feeble, but I'm never hungry!
New lotus leaves fill the clear pond—
how could you say that I have no new clothes?

Making Fun of Deviant Scholars

Those in this world who seek fame and profit
are shameless both in word and in deed.
In writing poems they admire "Yang the Fifth;"
their lives recall the monkeys who wanted "three at night."
In their teaching they do not encourage filial and fraternal piety;
their studies are not conducive to profundity of thought.
They love debating, outdoing Master Su;
they explain texts, distorting Hui-an's meaning.
They flatter you to your face, putting forth their artful lies;
their words are honeyed, fragrant and sweet.
I keep my mouth shut and preserve my Way:
I never deal with those vulgar scholars.

According to the biography of a certain Yang Hsiu in the *History of the Northern Dynasties* (*Pei Shih*), Yang had a younger brother named Chün-chih who "wrote many songs with six-word lines which became immensely popular, and were called 'p'an-lü songs by Yang the Fifth.' They were copied out and sold and there was a constant demand for them. Once, Chün-chih was passing through the market place when he picked up some of these texts to revise them, as he thought they contained errors in diction, but the bookseller said, 'Yang the Fifth was a sage of ancient times who wrote these songs. Who do you think you are to dare express an opinion about them!' Yang was greatly pleased." The point appears to be that the poetasters of Jōzan's time are also unable to distinguish between commercial popularity and real quality.

The Taoist philosopher Chuang Tzu tells a famous parable about a tribe of monkeys cared for by a monkey trainer. "When the monkey trainer was handing out acorns, he said, 'You get three in the morning and four at night.' This made all the monkeys furious. 'Well, then,' he said, 'you get four in the morning and three at night.' The monkeys were all delighted. There was no change in the reality behind the words and yet the monkeys responded with joy and anger" (translation by Burton Watson).

Master Su, or Su Ch'in, was a brilliant strategist of the Warring States Period; he was noted for his talent at persuasive rhetoric. Hui-an is Chu Hsi (1130–1200), the greatest thinker in Neo-Confucian philosophy, and the man who established a body of texts and interpretations that stood for centuries as the foundation of orthodoxy.

Reading the Poetry Collection of Master "Ishikawa" (Shih-ch'uan)

Master Shih-ch'uan was a man of the Ming dynasty. He was skilled at poetry, and has a collection which circulates in the world.

> We share the name of "Master Ishikawa";
> your fame as a poet shook the Great Ming.
> "All my life I've loved rivers and mountains!"
> These words express my feelings too.

The name Ishikawa, read "Shih-ch'uan" in Chinese, was Ishikawa Jōzan's surname. It was also the *hao* (pen name) of the minor Ming poet Yin Yun-hsiao (1480–1516), as Jōzan apparently discovered to his great delight. Yin belonged to a group of poets known as the Ten Talents.

Poem Chanted While Ill on a Summer Night

> My body fades, my years draw to their end.
> My mind is at peace as I lie awake at night.
> The calls of the frogs and the cries of the cuckoos
> mingled with the rain break over my sickbed.

On the Leopard-Leg

Poet's note: Commonly known as the "pile-dirt" or the *yabuka*. A type of mosquito.

> The leopard-leg is really hateful—
> how many people has it harmed?
> Without a sound, its beak attacks;
> poisonous, it causes wounds.
> Quickly it takes on mottled colors:
> now its guts look like embroidery!
> Living in the woods, it's difficult to escape this pest;
> every evening I can only scratch away!

Roosting Crows

> Day after day when evening comes
> flocks of them return, flashing as they fly.
> A *go* board from which white has retreated;
> a painting splashed with random block dots.

Eating Roasted Matsutake Mushrooms

You gather them in the shade of pine trees.
You don't boil them, you don't steam them.
Roast them over charcoals glowing red in the brazier:
like the cremation of little naked monks!

The mushrooms in question are *armillaria edodes.*

Walking Through the Mountains, Moved by an Old Tree

With withered cane, taking slow steps,
   I walk the blue-green slopes.
I linger by the flowers, and tug at my beard
   as I chant poems.
This old tree, tall and solitary,
   seems to be like me:
no blossom, no seed, no branch at all.

Impromptu

Early in the morning I sweep with tattered broom;
not a speck of dust remains along the path.
I sit so long I can watch the flowers bloom;
deep in the garden, the birds amuse themselves.
The stream's sound attracts no vulgar visitors—
the mountain colors are for this hermit alone.
Here, behind the humble gate,
the old plum tree is even skinnier than I.

Pomegranate Blossoms

The Queen Mother of the West planted them in her garden;
Chang Ch'ien transplanted them to the capital of Han.
The blossoms bloom, burning like fiery flames;
the seeds ripen, scattered bits of coral.

Chang Ch'ien was dispatched by a Han emperor to find horses in Central Asia. In popular mythology, he rode a raft to the source of the Yangtze River, where he encountered the goddess, Queen Mother of the West.

Five Poems

1.

The autumn mountains have many lovely scenes,
gods and spirits are everywhere you go.
Wash your mouth with stream water and brighten your smile;
push aside the clouds and sleep peacefully.

2.

Gold scales playfully swim among the reeds;
blue-green wings meander from the wood.
I leave the chanting of poems to the crickets;
my sick body passes another autumn.

3.

I wander at will both day and night,
the poems flowing forth in waves.
At peace by myself, no vulgar people near,
facing the green mountains with my head of white hair.

4.

The cicadas' chanting breaks over my lonely pillow,
as the cock crows, the lamp burns low.
Under the covers there's a hot-water lady
and so I can ignore the morning chill.

5.

A hundred years go by like a minute.
Ten thousand possessions become a pile of rubble.
In service or retirement I've lived through four emperors:
there's nothing I can do, and nothing I can't.

A "hot-water lady" is a type of foot warmer.

Recording a Dream on a Moonlit Night

The paper window starts to glow,
    as if dawn were near.
but sick as I am I'm much too lazy
    to gaze out at the autumn sky.
My dreaming soul is suddenly transformed
    into a flying immortal
who journeys straight past the Milky Way
    to the palace of the moon.

Inscribed on a Portrait of Tu Fu
Riding on Donkeyback

The servant shoulders drinking gourds and baggage:
"Where are you coming from?" "The Thatched Hut!"
Although he rode around on donkeyback,
is this not the man known as The King of Poetry?

According to *Miscellaneous Records of Immortals Among the Clouds* (a forged "T'ang" text actually dating from the early twelfth century), when Tu Fu was ten years old, he dreamed of a man who informed him that he, Tu Fu, was actually an official of the Star of Literature who had been exiled to earth to become a major writer of the T'ang dynasty. This man also told him where to find a magic stone with an inscription on it referring to Tu as "The King of Poetry."

Expressing My Feelings

By the eastern stream for years there's lived a hermit,
hiding his tracks, refusing visitors.
For long he has dwelt among the Poetry Immortals
and been a neighbor of the God of Poverty!
With bamboo mat and drinking gourd, he takes pleasure in the Way;
with pillow and cane he rests his body.
I own the treasure called "Lack of Greed":
it makes me richer than Millionaire Shih.

Millionaire Shih was Shih Ch'ung (249–300), a man famed for this wealth and extravagant lifestyle. The penultimate line refers to the *Tso Chuan,* a historical text of the third century B.C., which quotes a certain Tzu-kan as saying, "I consider lack of covetousness to be a treasure; you, Sir, consider jade to be a treasure" (Duke Hsiang, fifteenth year).

A Weeping Cherry Tree in the Garden

A tree with a thousand filaments,
    each twenty feet in length;
the profusion of blossoms hanging down,
    wafting subtle fragrance!
Had this tree grown in the Imperial Garden
    in the dynasty of T'ang
would Li Po ever have compared
    the Lady Yang to *hai-t'ang* flowers?

Li Po in a famous poem compared the beautiful visage of Yang Kuei-fei to flowers (he seems actually to have had peonies in mind, rather than *hai-t'ang*).

I sent a scroll of several of my poems to [Noma] Seiken and playfully inscribed this at the end of the scroll

> I've wanted to tell you my spring feelings but write few letters now—
> look back, and think of me among the cloudy peaks.
> Please don't tell the rich and powerful about these works of mine:
> these are the poems of a woodcutter in the hills.

Inscription for a Bamboo *Nyoi Scepter*

> Dragon's shape
> mind's expression
> a gentleman such as this
> in this world is rare

The third line may refer obliquely to a famous anecdote in which Wang Hui-chih, son of China's greatest calligrapher, Wang Hsi-chih, referred to his favorite plant, bamboo, as "This Gentleman." Sei Shōnagon, in her *Pillow Book,* relates an episode in which she achieved notoriety by alluding to this story.

Expressing My Feelings

> I've said farewell forever to worldly dust
>   and entered deep seclusion;
> I've forgotten what it means
>   to be honored or to be shamed.
> At midnight, beside the lamp,
>   for thirty springtimes now,
> what has intoxicated me has been not lovely skirts
>   but books.

Inscription for a Wooden Backscratcher

Poet's note: Also known as a claw-stick; commonly called "Ma-ku's hand"

> Carving quite extraordinary
> wherever I itch you bring relief
> a single scratch from the Immortal's hand
> and my old back feels wonderful

Ma-ku was a famous woman immortal in the Taoist pantheon. She lived as a hermit in the mountains.

Recording My Feelings in Old Age

My useless life has passed the eighty-year mark—
here I am, still roosting in the Ōtotsu Nest.
In planning life I take few medicines,
but in old age I do read lots of books.
I've enjoyed the pleasures of Jung Ch'i-ch'i,
though I cannot sing the song of Lin Lei yet.
My Tao-mind has forgotten worldly matters:
luckily, I've been able to avoid the wind and waves.

Lines 5 and 6 refer to two passages in *Lieh Tzu*. Jung Ch'i-ch'i tells "Confucius" that he has three pleasures: to have been born human, to have been born male, and to have lived to the age of ninety. Lin Lei, at the age of nearly a hundred, sang as he scavenged among the discarded grain left behind by the reapers. When "Confucius's" disciple Tzu-kung asked him why he should sing in the midst of such poverty, he responded that he was without wife or sons and thus had no burdens. He then went on to articulate a Taoist philosophy of death: "How do I know that life and death are not as good as each other? How do I know that it is not a delusion to crave anxiously for life?" Jōzan may be implying that he has not yet reached Lin Lei's state of total peace, while also alluding to his own age: around ninety, but not yet near one hundred.

Inscribed on the Wall of the Toyokuni Shrine

Dilapidated, this old shrine of the eastern mountains;
green moss and twisting vines cling to the ruined walls.
The hero's spirit has flown away—no priest makes offerings;
the autumn moon and spring wind have taken over now.

The shrine was located in the Higashiyama district of Kyoto, and was dedicated to Toyotomi Hideyoshi (1536–98), who in 1599 had been apotheosized as Toyokuni Diamyōjin.

Experiencing Joy

In this mountain village, it is the ancient springtime—
I sleep serenely in the valley of clouds.
No wife and children burden my home;
my mind feels the joy of the immortals.
The bamboo cane is a three-foot dragon;
on the pine-wood bed lies a thousand year-old crane.
The old man of the Lesser Cave Paradise
touches creation and chants poems to himself.

The Lesser Cave Paradise (*hsiao yu tung*) was the name of a Taoist sacred cave in China which Jōzan adopted as one of his pen names. The three characters, read *Shoyudō* in Japanese, are inscribed on a wooden plaque above the entrance to the Shisendō.

Leaning on My Cane

Leaning on my cane within the woods—
shrine trees soaring high all around.
A dog barks at the heels of a beggar;
an ox plows the field, a farmer behind.
My life—the cold stream water;
old, sick—sunset in the sky.
I've known to the full the joys of mist and cloud:
ten years away from a century of life!

Inscription for a Fantastic Bamboo Nyoi Scepter

Ah, *nyoi* of bamboo!
Elephant's trunk, dragon's shape
held in the hands of Confucian scholars
also by martial officers
hollow down the center to express
clarity of mind
How could I use you merely to scratch my back?

Jōzan owned two *nyoi* ("as you like it") scepters (symbols of authority or scholarly and spiritual attainment) which he dubbed the Greater and Lesser Dragons.

Self-Eulogy on His Birthday Portrait as Painted by Kanō Tanyū

Nyoi in hand, leaning on armrest,
wearing dark robe and black cap.
Silent is his noble visage;
brilliant is his spirit.
He communicates with the Creator
and nurtures the Tao within.
A stubborn old man now eighty years old,
a hermit of three-fold yang.
And who is this hermit, you may ask?
The Mountain Man of the Thirty-Six!

"Three-fold yang" means very strong yang (as opposed to yin) power. The Thirty-Six, of course, are the Poetry Immortals.

Poems by the Thirty-six Chinese Poets Selected by Ishikawa Jōzan

Su Wu (140?–70 B.C.)
Parting of Brothers

Flesh and bone are leaves upon the branch;
those joined in friendship are also very close.
Within the four seas, all men are brothers:
Who need be a stranger on the road?
How much more us, trees that share a branch,
as if I had the same body as you!
In the past we were like duck and drake,
now apart, like Antares and Orion in the sky.

SU WU was a Chinese envoy to the Hsiung-nu nomads, held captive by them for nineteen years. He returned to China in 81 B.C. Already in the Sung dynasty, Su Shih (1037–1101) had cast doubt on the authenticity of the poems attributed to him, and it has been assumed ever since that they were in all likelihood pastiches of the late Han or the Six Dynasties periods. Nevertheless, these poems and others attributed to Su's friend and supporter, Li Ling, were frequently cited as early examples of "five-word" verse (i.e., poems with five monosyllabic words per line).

T'ao Ch'ien (365–427)
Miscellaneous Poem

I built my hut where people live
yet there is no racket of horse and carriage.
"I ask you, Sir, how is that possible?"
When the mind is distant, the place becomes remote.
I pluck chrysanthemums beneath the eastern hedge,
look longingly at the southern mountains.
The mountain air is lovely at sunset;
birds in flight two by two return.
In these things there lies a subtle meaning:
I would convey it, but I've lost the words.

T'AO CH'IEN (T'ao Yüan-ming) was the first great nature poet, one of the greatest of all Chinese poets, and an exemplar of the gentleman-scholar in retirement from government service. The great T'ang-dynasty masters drew inspiration from his work. This is the fifth poem in from the series *Drinking Wine*.

Hsieh Ling-yun (385–433)
Climbing the Tower on the Pond

Fresh weather transforms the lingering winter winds;
new yang-force takes over from old yin.
The pond-bank puts forth springtime plants;
the garden willows fill with singing birds.
"Flourish, flourish": I grieve at that Ode of Pin;
"Fulsome, fulsome": I'm moved by that song of Ch'u!
Living alone, how easily time prolongs;
apart from crowds, it's hard to brood within.
Was it only in antiquity that men had self-control?
"Withdrawing and being free of care" is proved again today.

HSIEH LING-YUN was the second great nature poet after T'ao Ch'ien. He combines extensive landscape imagery—often depicting a more secluded, wilder nature than in T'ao—with dense allusiveness. The present poem includes both Hsieh's most famous couplet ("The pond-bank," etc.), frequently quoted by later scholars, and a complex web of allusions to such classic texts as the *Ch'u Tz'u, Shih Ching, Li Chi, Ku-liang Commentary to the Spring and Autumn Annals,* and *I Ching.*

Pao Chao (412?–66)
In the Manner of Liu Kung-kan

Barbarian winds blow down northern snow,
a thousand miles crossing Dragon Mountain.
A gathering of gentlemen at Jasper Terrace:
flying dancers before the pair of pillars!
At such a time, some men craft their own beauty,
avoiding the season when the year turns warm.
In that warmth, the peach blossom and plum
are pure and clean and do not flaunt their looks.

PAO CHAO was a poet of courtly elegance, interweaving elegiac melancholy and rich imagery bordering upon the decadent. This poem of his, like others, may contain political allegory (Jasper Terrace was built by a tyrant of the past). If so, the "peach blossom and plum" may be seen as symbols for men of integrity who hold themselves aloof from regimes unworthy of their service. Liu Kung-kan refers to the poet Liu Chen (d. 217).

Tu Shen-yen (d. after 705)

Written in response to an imperial request to compose a poem on the
Chung-nan Mountains while in attendance at a banquet in the Three Palaces
of the Paradise Islands

> The Northern Dipper hangs by the city wall;
> the Southern Mountains slant athwart the palace.
> At the tips of clouds, gold towers stand far off;
> from tree tops, jade chambers now hang!
> Halfway across the ridge, fine vapors flow;
> the central peak is circled by auspicious mist.
> This humble official offers his longevity poem:
> forever here to honor Emperor Yao!

TU SHEN-YEN was the grandfather of the great Tu Fu (712–70) and himself a major early
T'ang court poet, master of the tight diction and flowery rhetoric characteristic of the style. The
present poem is a birthday offering to the emperor—the Chung-nan (or southern) Mountains
are a frequently used image of longevity.

Ch'en Tzu-ang (661–702)
Moved By What I Encounter

> The Sage seeks not to profit Self;
> his worry lies in succoring the folk.
> The "Yellow Canopy" was no concern of Yao's;
> what need to speak of the Jasper Terrace!
> But I have heard of a western teaching
> whose Way of Purity is honored more and more.
> Why is it then that they use gold and jade
> to carve into images which they so adore?
> Cloud-capped temples exhaust the mountain woods;
> precious paintings, pearls and feathers exercise their thoughts.
> Even demons could not do such work;
> how can human artistry suffice?
> Boasting vainly, their worldly ties increase;
> they pride themselves on wisdom—their Way grows darker still.

CH'EN TZU-ANG, like Tu Shen-yen a major early T'ang poet, is best known for his ambitious
series of thirty eight poems entitled *Kan-yü* ("Moved By What I Encounter"), of which this is
the nineteenth. As Stephen Owen writes in his book, *The Poetry of the Early T'ang* (New Haven:
Yale University Press, 1977, 199–200), this poem is "genuinely caustic in its attack on Buddhist

secular wealth," even though others in the series do seem sympathetic to Buddhism as such. Owen also points out that "Empress Wu (r. 684–704) was particularly devoted to Buddhism, and the poem may be topical rather than a general attack on Buddhist secular wealth." The third and fourth lines mean that a true sage-emperor like Yao was not interested in the external trappings of power. (On the painting of Ch'en Tzu-ang at the Shisendō, only the first four lines are inscribed.)

Li Po (701–62)
Ancient Air

The Great Elegance has been defunct for ages:
when I have faded, who will plead its cause?
The Kingly Way was choked with vines and weeds;
the Warring States were full of bramble-thorns!
Dragons and tigers bit each other;
the swords and spears continued to wild Ch'in.
By then, how faint the orthodox voice had grown;
grief and sorrow moved the poets of *Sao*.
Yang and Ma revitalized the sluggish flow,
opening a stream that rushed forth without bound.
Though rise and fall go through ten thousand changes,
the classic works have truly sunk from view.
The writings after Chien-an up to now
are merely lovely—not worthy of true praise.
But our sage time has restored antiquity:
his robes calmly hanging, the Emperor prizes the pure and true.
Men of talent are drawn to this reign of peace and enlightenment:
riding the tide, they leap to glory!
Style and substance mutually illuminate;
a myriad stars twinkle in the autumnal vault.
My own intention lies in editing and transmitting
so the glory can scintillate for another thousand springs.
Should I be successful in emulating the Sage
I too would rest my brush where they "catch the unicorn."

LI PO, together with Tu Fu, is usually considered one of the two greatest poets of China. Often his free-wheeling, "romantic" tendencies are contrasted with Tu Fu's sterner social conscious-ness, but a more careful reading of Li Po reveals him to have been a more complex figure than this. The present poem, the first of a series of fifty-nine with the same title, shows that Li, like Tu, was concerned about what he considered to be the general degeneration in the course of history of the Confucian literary tradition (although with periods of revival, which Li considers his own period to be). Li claims that he wants to "edit and transmit" works of importance, as the Sage—Confucius himself—had done, and to set aside his brush upon hearing, like Confucius again, the report of the capture of a unicorn (an omen of the coming of an enlightened monarch). The *Li Sao* was the masterpiece of Ch'ü Yuan (343?–278 B.C.), China's first great poet. Ssu-ma Hsiang-ju (179–117 B.C.) and Yang Hsiung (53 B.C.–A.D. 18)—the "Yang and Ma" of the poem—were two great masters of Han-dynasty literature. The Chien-an period (196–220) was noted for the vigor of its poetry.

Tu Fu (712–70)
Climbing Yueh-yang Tower

In past I heard of Tung-t'ing Lake;
today I climb the Yueh-yang Tower.
Wu and Ch'u to east and south here split;
yang and yin both day and night do float.
From friends or family—not a single word;
old and sick, in a solitary boat. . . .
Horses of war fight north of mountain passes:
I lean on the railing, weeping tears that flow.

TU FU, usually considered China's greatest poet, had at least two significant stylistic manners: in one, he used simple, straightforward diction to express his feelings or to describe the effects of warfare on the common people, while in the other, he used a more fragmented, complex diction to create a multileveled world in which history, mythology, and his own personal experience are linked and contrasted. Tu Fu wrote *Climbing Yueh-yang Tower* in 768; the tower commands a magnificent view of China's most famous lake, Tung-t'ing, in the northern part of Hunan province.

Wang Wei (701–61)
The Estate at Chung-nan

In middle age I've come to love the Tao;
late in life, I settle beneath South Mountain.
When inspiration comes I walk alone;
the finest views I keep all to myself.
I reach the spot where the stream runs out,
sit and watch the hour when clouds arise.
Sometimes I encounter an old woodcutter:
talking, laughing, putting off return.

WANG WEI was the quintessential Chinese nature poet, as well as being a painter later regarded as the founder of the "Southern" or literati school of painting. In his poetry, Wang represents tranquil nature scenes tinged with sadness but also with a Buddhist-influenced sense of transcendence that borders upon the religious.

Meng Hao-jan (689–740)
At Year's End Returning to Southern Mountain

At northern tower, done with submitting papers;
in Southern Mountain, I return to my humble hut.
Untalented, rejected by a wise sovereign;
very ill, avoided by old friends.
White hairs press me to old age;
the vernal yang-force hastens out the year.
Full of feeling, sad, I cannot sleep;
the pine-moon at night shines through an empty window.

MENG HAO-JAN, like Wang Wei—with whom he was often paired—was a great master of nature imagery which he tends to convey through the use of a densely textured, high-toned diction derived from such Six Dynasties masters as Hsieh Ling-yun.

Kao Shih (702?–65)
The Double-Yang Festival

The season's changes startle me,
    my temples blossom white;
in vain I circle the eastern hedge—
    no flowers have opened there.
My hundred years are nearly half-gone,
    I've been "thrice fired" from jobs;
My five acres are all overgrown,
    I'm stranded at heaven's edge.
Does any "white-robe" visit here,
    knocking at my door?
I too wear a cap of black,
    precarious on my head.
I really have come to "sit alone
    and vaguely scratch my head;"
the gateway willows sigh sadly,
    amidst the cawing of evening crows.

KAO SHIH was one of the finest poets of the High T'ang period, the golden age of Chinese poetry. It has long been recognized, however, that this poem was in fact written by the minor Sung poet, Ch'eng Chü (1078–1144). The penultimate line does contain a witty allusion to a poem actually by Kao Shih, entitled *On the Ninth Day of the Ninth Month—In Response to the Shao-fu, Yen,* which ends with the couplet: "Even if I did climb high, it would only break my heart / best to sit alone and vaguely scratch my head." "Climbing high" (i.e., to mountain lookouts and other scenic spots) was one of the favorite ways to celebrate the autumn festival of the ninth day of the ninth lunar month (the "Double Ninth" or "Double-Yang" festival). Chrysanthemums were also associated with this occasion. T'ao's Ch'ien's love for them was famous; he plucked them by the "eastern hedge" according to his famous fifth poem from the series *Drinking Wine,* the very poem chosen by Jōzan to represent T'ao (see above). It was also T'ao who was once brought wine by a visitor in a "white robe." Another incident alluded to in this poem is that of Meng Chia, who is said to have become so inebriated at a Double Ninth celebration that when the wind blew his black cap off his head he did not notice at all.

The poet here emphasizes not the usual joy of the Double-Yang Festival but his feelings of personal sadness and professional disappointment.

Ts'en Shen (715–70)
Inscribed on the West Tower at Kuo-chou

I've made a mess of my entire life,
stumbling along—and now my hair's all white.
Wherever I've gone I've been a failure;
my wife and children should be ashamed of me.
Although my enlightened Lord has cast me off
my heart of loyalty will never cease.
Sadness comes and I've nowhere to go
except to climb the prefecture's west tower.

TS'EN SHEN was a friend of Kao Shih, and like him was one of the finest poets of the golden age after Tu Fu, Li Po and Wang Wei.

Ch'u Kuang-hsi (fl. 742)
Flowing Waterfall in Mountains

In the mountains there is flowing water;
if you ask, I do not know its name.
It reflects on earth the sky's color;
flies high into roaring rain.
It turns, and the deep ravine is filled;
divides, and levels off the tarn.
Calm and lucid, seen by no man,
year after year quite pure.

CH'U KUANG-HSI was a relatively little-known nature poet resembling Wang Wei and Meng Hao-jan in his emphasis on the theme of reclusion. The "table and cane" mentioned in the final line are items with which to serve one's parents or elders. Also referred to are the two great classic anthologies of poetry, the *Shih Ching* (of which *Feng* is a major division) and the *Ch'u Tz'u* (in which the *Li Sao* by Ch'ü Yuan is the most famous poem). The second line contains yet another reference to the fifth poem of T'ao Ch'ien's *Drinking Wine* series.

Wang Ch'ang-ling (d. 756)
The Palace of Eternal Faithfulness

On *wu-t'ung* trees by the golden well
  autumn leaves turn yellow;
the pearl curtain hangs unrolled,
  frost falls in the night.
With bed-warmer on jade pillow,
  face all drained of color,
she lies and listens to the south palace waterclock
  drip clearly through the night.

WANG CH'ANG-LING was once regarded as one of the supreme poetic geniuses of the T'ang. His writings on poetic theory were also widely read and were introduced in Japan by Kūkai, who quoted extensively from them.

Wei Ying-wu (c.736–c.792)
Sent to a Taoist on Ch'üan-chiao Mountain

This morning the office studio is cold;
suddenly I think of my friend up in the mountains.
At the bottom of gulleys, gathering brambles for fires;
returning to boil white pebbles for his meal.
I want to take a gourdful of wine
far off to comfort him on evenings of windswept rain.
But falling leaves carpet the deserted mountain:
where could I follow any of his tracks?

WEI YING-WU was a figure of great importance in mid-T'ang poetry, second only to Po Chü-i and Han Yü (see below) in his influence on later generations and on poets of the Sung dynasty. The range of his subject matter is broad, from highly personal poems of lamentation on the death of his wife to delicate nature poems such as this famous anthology piece.

Han Yu (768–824)
Song of Being Secreted in Prison

My eyes are darkened,
  I squint, I'm blind!
My ears are humming,
  I cannot hear a sound.
Mornings no sunrise,
  nights no moon or stars;

Do I know or not know,
  am I dead or alive?
My crime must be punished,
  the Heavenly King is sage and wise.

HAN YÜ is a towering figure in the history of Chinese thought and literature. He attempted to spark a Confucian revival after what he saw as centuries of increasing Buddhist dominance, but his efforts were only to be met with a sympathetic response centuries after his death when Ou-yang Hsiu (see below) would declare him to have been the forerunner of the Sung Confucian renaissance. This poem is one of ten songs for the *ch'in,* a plucked-string instrument resembling a zither loved by the Chinese literati. The theme is the imprisonment of the virtuous King Wen by the evil Emperor Chou of the Shang dynasty in antiquity.

Liu Chang-ch'ing (709–80?)
Early Spring in the Ocean Salt Headquarters

A minor official in this little seaside town,
at New Year's a white-haired old man.
This one post makes me a distant traveler;
ten thousand affairs seem floating tumbleweed.
Willows color within the lonely walls;
orioles sound through the fragile rain.
My wanderer's heart was already broken:
who needed to add the winds of spring?

LIU CHANG-CH'ING was another great T'ang master whose name ranks just below those of Tu Fu, Li Po, and Wang Wei. Liu was particularly noted for his finely crafted, resonant couplets which are often cited independently in the later critical literature as beautiful miniature landscape scenes. The third couplet of this poem is a good example of Liu's elegant touch.

Liu Tsung-yuan (773–819)
The Old Fisherman

The old fisherman at night
  sleeps beneath the western cliff;
at dawn he draws pure Hsiang River water
  and boils it on a fire of Ch'u bamboo.
As mist evaporates and the sun appears
  no one is in view;
"creak" goes his boat—the mountain and river
  turn green.

Looking back from the horizon
  as he follows the middle flow,
above the cliff without a thought
  the clouds each other pursue.

LIU TSUNG-YUAN was a friend of Han Yü and like him a master of both poetry and prose. His travel essays were pioneering works in the important *yu-chi* ("travel account") genre.

Liu Yü-hsi (772–842)
The Temple of the Mysterious Capital

Along the purple road, red dust
  brushes our faces;
not a single man but says,
  "We're back from seeing the flowers!"
At the Temple of the Mysterious Capital,
  a thousand peach blossom trees,
all of them planted after Master Liu took leave.

LIU YÜ-HSI was a close friend of Po Chü-i (see below) and one of the greatest poets of the mid-T'ang period.

Po Chü-i (772–846)
Song of Wang Chao-chün—Song of the Brilliant Concubine

The Han envoy is sent back—a message goes with him:
"Whenever will mere gold redeem the moth-eyed beauty!
If the Emperor should inquire about her lovely face,
don't say that she's less beautiful now than when living in his palace!"

PO CHÜ-I was the most popular and widely read of all Chinese poets in Japan. Sugawara no Michizane (845–903) modeled the style of his accomplished Chinese verse on that of Po. The present poem is based on the famous story of Wang Chao-chun, sent in marriage by a Han emperor to the Khan of the Hsiung-nu nomads because the emperor had been misled to believe she was not particularly beautiful (she had refused to bribe the court painter whose portraits were being used as the basis of decision). The poem refers to the regretful emperor's unsuccessful attempt to ransom her later.

Li Ho (791–817)
Ballad of the Prefect of Goose Gate

Black clouds press on city walls,
  walls about to crumble;
chain-mail glitters in the sun,
  golden scales spread out.

Sounds of trumpets fill the sky
    in the autumn colors;
above the frontier—northern rouge—
    congeals the purple of night.
Half unfurled, our banners of red
    approach the River I;
frost weighing heavy, muffled drumbeats
    do not carry in the cold.
To repay our sovereign for his trust
    at the Tower of Yellow Gold
jade dragons clasped within our hands
    we die now for our lord.

LI HO, the "ghostly talent," is one of the strangest figures in the history of Chinese literature. His bizarre, ambiguous poems are filled with imagery of warfare, death, and the supernatural.

Lu T'ung (d. 835)
People's Day: The Establishment of Spring

Spring passes, spring returns,
    unlimited the spring!
This morning for the very first time
    I feel I've become a man.
From this day on the goal of "Conquering Self"
    seems quite attainable;
my complexion and the plum blossoms,
    both renewed today.

LU T'UNG was an eccentric poet of the Han Yü circle best known for his strange, lengthy poem on an eclipse of the moon. Here he plays on the coincidental concurrence of "People's (or Man's) Day"—the seventh day of the new lunar year—and the Establishment of Spring (li-ch'un), the official beginning of the spring season.

Tu Mu (803–52)
Traveling Early

I drop my whip, let my horse go as he will;
miles we travel before the rooster crows.
Beneath the woods, I carry scraps of dreams;
the leaves twirl, suddenly startling me awake.
Frost congeals—a lonely goose returns;
moonlit dawn—distant mountains slant.

Servant-boy, do not complain of hardship:
when have the paths of life ever been free of care?

TU MU, dubbed "Lesser Tu" by contrast with Tu Fu, is known for his romantic entanglements
with singing girls and for his poignant poetry, much of it on the theme of travel.

Li Shang-yin (813?–58)
The Well Rope

The Well Rope and T'ien-p'eng Mountain
  in the palm of a single hand!
A vain boast, that Heaven set a sword here
  as a peak!
The Eightfold Maze clusters to the east
  at the mouth of Swallow River;
watchmen's clappers hang in the west,
  from pines on snowy peaks.
How lamentable, that king of old
  who turned into a cuckoo;
perhaps the founding ruler was a true dragon
  after all.
For future times, let us inform
  the heroes of treachery:
please do not come down Gold Ox Road
  to retrace ancient steps.

LI SHANG-YIN, a major late T'ang poet, may well be the most difficult and obscure writer in
Chinese poetry. Jōzan has chosen a poem which even for Li must be considered impenetrable.
In general, if we follow the scholar Yü Pi-yun, it may be interpreted as a warning that the
natural defenses and rugged terrain of Szechwan province in western China render it an
unwise spot for ambitious warlords either to invade or to use as a staging ground for rebellion.
The Well Rope is a constellation; the other references have to do with Szechwan's history,
mythology, and geography.

Ling-ch'e (746–816)
Staying Overnight at East Forest Temple

Weather cold, ferocious tigers
  roar from cliffside caves;
beneath the trees, no man at all,
  only the moon is here.

For a thousand years they taught the School of Symbols,
    now nothing is heard of it:
the incense that they burn today
    is to please the ghosts and spirits.

LING-CH'E, a Buddhist monk, is an important representative of the monk-poets of the T'ang who associated with Confucian scholars and exchanged poetry with them. The poems of these men sometimes refer to Buddhism (the "School of Symbols") but sometimes bear no relationship to the poet's monastic vocation. The final two lines of this poem may be interpreted to mean that true Buddhism is no longer practiced at this particular temple, only a debased, superstitious cult.

Han Shan (early ninth century)
In the Style of the Ch'u Tz'u

A true man, ah! on a mountain path,
    clouds curl about him, ah! mists for hat strings.
He holds a fragrant flower, ah! wishes to offer it,
    but the road is distant, ah! and hard to travel.
Heart frustrated, ah! and in confusion,
    indeed he stands alone, ah! loyal and pure.

HAN SHAN was a semi-legendary Ch'an (Zen) Buddhist eccentric. The three hundred some-odd poems attributed to him show signs of having been written by at least two different hands. Some of them are virtual sermons in verse; others are brilliant nature poems which convey Buddhist meaning through landscape. The poem chosen by Jōzan to represent Han Shan, although actually uncharacteristic of either type, is for some reason the single most frequently quoted Han Shan poem in the Chinese critical literature known as *shih-hua* ("talks on poetry"). It emulates the unique style of the ancient anthology known as the *Songs of Ch'u* (*Ch'u Tz'u*).

Lin Pu (967–1028)

I built a [longevity] hall for myself and have written this quatrain to commemorate it

    Around the lake, green mountains
        face my humble hut;
    before the tomb, the bamboo grove
        grows withered and sparse.
    In case one day a messenger
        should seek my writings at Mao-ling

> I can take joy in never having written
> a *Book on the Imperial Sacrifice*.

LIN PU was a recluse who lived by himself at West lake near Hangchou. Because of his delicate, refined poems about the place, West Lake's fame as a poetic retreat became firmly established. Lin can be seen as second only to T'ao Ch'ien as an exemplar for Jōzan of the scholarly poet-recluse. A "longevity hall" was a gravesite prepared while the individual was still alive. The last two lines of this poem are based on an episode from the biography of the great Han-dynasty court poet, Ssu-ma Hsiang-ju (179–117 B.C.) in the *Shih Chi* (*Records of the Historian*) by China's most reknown writer of history, Ssu-ma Ch'ien (c.145–c.85 B.C.). The emperor, concerned that Ssu-ma Hsiang-ju was seriously ill, sent a messenger to his residence at Mao-ling to gather and preserve any writings of his that may not yet have been received at court. Upon arrival, the messenger discovered that Ssu-ma Hsiang-ju had already passed away. The poet's wife presented to the messenger the only remaining uncollected work of Hsiang-ju's, the *Book on the Imperial Sacrifice*. Lin Pu prides himself on never having written such a work, that is to say, a book involved with affairs of state, toward which he professes complete indifference.

Shao Yung (1012–77)
Head-and-Tail Song

It's not that Yao-fu loves writing poetry;
he may be old, but his spirit has not died!
The pure tranquility of water and bamboo I've occupied long since;
prosperity, high station of oriole and blossom, these I do possess!
The moon in the *wu-t'ung* trees illuminates my heart;
the breeze among the willows comes and blows upon my face.
Embraced this way by such serenity,
it's not that Yao-fu loves writing poetry.

SHAO YUNG (Yao-fu) was an eccentric Neo-Confucian thinker who created a bizarre system of numerology. He also wrote highly idiosyncratic poetry sequences and created the "Head-and-Tail" genre in which the first line of a poem (the "head") is repeated verbatim as the final line (the "tail"). As Yamamoto Shirō has suggested, the meaning of the opening and closing line of the example selected by Jōzan may be that although Shao Yung does not particularly like to write poetry, the poems seem to come to him naturally.

Mei Yao-ch'en (1002–60)
Gold Mountain Temple

After this Wu traveler has come alone,
the Ch'u boat returns in evening sunlight.
Mountain shapes disconnected from the land;
temple precincts reach right to the waves.
Nesting hawks—why don't they seek for prey?
Tame gulls form flocks, totally at peace.

The old monks here forget the months and years;
sitting on rocks they watch the river clouds.

MEI YAO-CH'EN, close friend of Ou-yang Hsiu (see below), was one of the leading architects
of a new poetry and poetics for the Sung dynasty. Gold Mountain Temple, located on an island
in the Yangtze River (which has since become connected to the riverbank) was considered one
of the most scenic locations in China. In a lengthy prose preface omitted by Jōzan, Mei relates
that birds of prey and other wild creatures miraculously avoided hunting on this holy spot and
on the nearby mountains. He also tells of a male and female seahawk which nested and raised
fledglings on the island.

Su Shun-ch'in (1008–48)
On the Mid-Autumn Festival Viewing the Moon
From New Bridge at Sung River—Echoing [a Poem by] Liu Ling

The moon illuminates the Yangtze River
    above and reflected below;
the painted bridge slants and cuts
    through the chilly light.
Among the clouds, lovely, lovely
    opens a golden cake;
on the waters, heavy, heavy
    sleeps a color-rainbow.
Master Buddha knows how to create
    a silvery universe;
innumerable immortals reside
    within this Jade Flower Palace.
The place is mighty, the scene transcendent,
    words will not suffice:
I only wish I could pursue it
    riding the winds of dawn.

SU SHUN-CH'IN, together with Mei Yao-ch'en (see above) and Ou-yang Hsiu (see below) was
one of the three greatest poets of his generation, the generation that set a new tone for poetry in
the Sung dynasty.

Ou-yang Hsiu (1007–72)
Sent to T'ien Yuan-chün of Ch'in-chou

From ancient times the frontier generals
    employed Confucian scholars
and thus they used their awesome fame
    to nurture the troops of Han.

Ten thousand horses—not one neighs,
    they listen to commands;
barbarian tribesmen—nothing to do
    but plow and weed the fields.
In dream you return to the tent at night,
    where you heard the flutes of the Ch'iang;
your poems recall the lookout tower,
    facing the clouds of the steppes.
Do not forget at Chen-yang
    you've left much love for you:
the peaches and plums at Northern Pond
    are flourishing just now.

OU-YANG HSIU was the chief scholar-statesman of his time, a great political and philosophical thinker who spearheaded the Neo-Confucian revival which was one of the Sung dynasty's major contributions to later Chinese culture and even to Korean and Japanese intellectual history. He was also a fine poet in a wide range of styles.

Su Shih (1037–1101)
After Snowfall—Inscribed on the Wall of the Northern Terrace

Above the city wall the early sun
    startles up the crows;
along the roads clear-weather mud
    already sinks carriage wheels.
Locked in ice this tower of jade—
    the cold gives us goose-bumps;
trembling in light the ocean of silver
    dazzles the eye into flower!
Locust larvae penetrate earth,
    at least a thousand feet;
germinating wheat like clustering clouds,
    how many farmers' fields!
Old and sick I lament
    I'm losing the strength to write poems:
in vain I chant the *Icicle Poem*
    thinking of old Liu Ch'a.

SU SHIH is usually considered to have been the greatest poet of the Sung dynasty. He and his circle of followers virtually created the literati ideal of the poet-painter-calligrapher. Liu Ch'a was a follower of Han Yü (see above) and was said to have been a drunkard and a murderer. The *Icicle Poem* is one of his few known works.

Huang T'ing-chien (1045–1105)
*Following the Rhymes of Yang Ming-shu's
Poems Offered in Parting*

In old age, I'm made prefect of T'ung-an:
my feet so weak, truly a convenient post!
But in my breast there is no "water mirror":
dare I accept appointment to the Ministry of Personnel?
I resent the existence of my empty fame—
still not escaped from worldly entanglements!
I dream I go off as a white seagull
over Chiang-nan where water looks like sky.

HUANG T'ING-CHIEN was one of the members of the Su Shih circle (see above), and himself a leading Sung poet and brilliant calligrapher. His poetry is highly allusive and densely textured, making him one of the more difficult Chinese poets. In the present poem, Huang expresses relief at an appointment as prefect of a provincial locality because his feet are hurting him and he would not find it convenient to stand for lengthy periods of time and to bow frequently as would be required at court. But he also begs out of a position as assistant office chief in the Ministry of Personnel.

Ch'en Shih-tao (1053–1101)
The Concubine's Lot is Poor

My master's house has twelve stories,
and there he treated me as if I were three thousand women!
From ancient times, the concubine's lot is poor:
I could not serve my master all my years.
I stood to dance and wish him a long life,
then had to escort him down Nan-yang funeral road.
Can I bear to don the clothes my lord gave me
to deck myself in spring finery for people now?
I would wail, the sound should reach the sky;
I would weep, the tears should reach the Springs.
But I fear the dead lack consciousness:
alone, I will ever feel this grief.

CH'EN SHIH-TAO, like Huang T'ing-chien (see above) a difficult, allusive poet, here compares himself to a concubine lamenting the death of her master. The "master" refers to Ch'en's teacher, the great writer of prose, Tseng Kung (1019–83), who had just died.

Ch'en Yü-i (1090–1138)
Ink Plum Blossom

So scintillating, lovely, in Chiang-nan
    ten thousand girls of jade:
since I left there, how many times
    have I seen them return in spring?
Now I meet them in the capital,
    and they're the same as ever,
except, alas! some blackened dust
    has soiled their white silk robes.

CH'EN YÜ-I was a transitional poet who bridged the gap between the expansive northern Sung and the more intimate southern Sung styles. Here, he compares both real plum blossoms and the plum blossoms in an ink painting to beautiful women.

Tseng Chi (1084–1166)
We moved within the city walls for protection from the rebels—the wind and rain were frigid, so Cheng Chien-tao made me a gift of wine

Misty rain, dark and damp,
    plums in the second month;
my whole family evades the rebels,
    lodges in this corner of the city.
Wishing to leave and go in search
    of the Executive of the Empyrean,
suddenly I'm honored by the arrival
    of the Administrator of Ch'ing Province!
I set my wife and children
    to washing out the cups;
I think of you with your brothers—
    passing drinks back and forth!
How can I live forever here,
    mired in depression?
Soon I will return along
    the pine path to Tea Mountain.

TSENG CHI, self-styled "The Recluse of Tea Mountain," was an important forerunner of the great Southern Sung masters, especially his devoted student in poetry, Lu Yu (1125–1210). In this poem, the "Executive of the Empyrean" was a Taoist immortal appointed to this exalted office by Lao Tzu, the semi-mythical author of the classic *Tao Te Ching*. The "Administrator of Ch'ing Province" is, by an elaborate play of words, a personification of wine.

Selected Bibliography

Chaves, Jonathan, " 'The Panoply of Images:' A Reconsideration of the Literary Theory of the Kung-an School." In Susan Bush and Christian Murck, eds., *Theories of the Arts in China* (Princeton: Princeton University Press, 1983) 341–64. For developments in late-Ming literary theory.

————. *The Columbia Book of Later Chinese Poetry.* (New York: Columbia University Press, 1986). For selected poems of the Ming and Ch'ing dynasties by poets of both the Archaist and Individualist schools, including Ch'ien Ch'ien-i and Yuan Hung-tao.

Chou, Chih-p'ing. *Yuan Hung-tao and the Kung-an School.* (Cambridge: Cambridge University Press, 1988). More on late-Ming literary theory and practice in China.

Matsushita Tadashi. *Edo Jidai no Shifu Shiron* [Kanshi Style and Theory in the Edo Period] (Tokyo: Meiji Shoin, 1969), 261–76. The best available discussion of Jōzan's poetic theory.

Watson, Burton. *Grass Hill: Poems and Prose by the Japanese Monk Gensei* (New York: Columbia University Press, 1983). Introduction, especially pages xxii-xxix for the interrelationships of Gensei, Jōzan, and Ch'en Yuan-yun.

————. *Japanese Literature in Chinese,* 1 and 2. (New York and London: Columbia University Press, 1975 and 1976).

————. *Kanshi: The Poetry of Ishikawa Jōzan and Other Edo-Period Poets.* (San Francisco: North Point Press, 1990). Contains translations of twenty-five poems by Jōzan.

Sources for the Poems of Ishikawa Jōzan

Page references noted SF are those of the 1676 edition of Jōzan's writings, the *Shimben Fushōshū*; Z refers to the *Zokushū* section of this work. F refers to the *Fushōshū*, the 1671 edition. Numbers before the solidus (/) refer to chapters of the edition; numbers after refer to pages, verso (a) and recto (b).

The Calligraphy of Ishikawa Jōzan
Stephen Addiss

The experience of the Shisendō is not limited to viewing its elegantly rustic poetry hall and the surrounding gardens. An even more personal form of art puts us in the presence of Jōzan himself, and that art is his unique calligraphy. Carved into wood at the gateway, inscribed on the portraits of the immortal poets, hanging in a set of three scrolls in the main tokonoma, and framed in several different rooms of the Shisendō, Jōzan's personal touch is visible to us today through his brushwork.

In East Asia it has long been believed that the sensitive viewer can learn a great deal about a person through calligraphy, the traces of human spirit that remain on paper and silk. No matter what the words may say, the hand that wields the brush cannot lie. Judging only from historical records, Jōzan remains a mysterious figure; why did he leave the service of the Tokugawa Shogunate and become the first true Chinese-style literatus in Japanese history? Documents alone can never answer this question. Viewing Jōzan's art, however, we can sense the inner character of the man.

Jōzan did not seem to have found a comfortable place for himself in the world of seventeenth-century Japan until he created his own persona as an artistic recluse in his own environment, the Shisendō. Deeply immersed in Chinese literati culture, he became a scholar-sage, passing his days with old books, poetry, calligraphy, and his ever-changing garden. He even emulated the Chinese scholar's musical inclinations, owning a seven-string *ch'in* (plate 44), the zither beloved by Chinese poets for its quiet, deep, meditative music. Furthermore, through the style in which he wrote poetry, signboards, plaques, and inscriptions, Jōzan set the stage for the revival of interest in *karayō,* the Chinese-influenced calligraphy that was to become a major force in Edo-period art. In his brushwork, as in every other facet of his life, Jōzan exemplified the values of the Sinophile scholar-poet-artist, adding a subtle

Japanese flavor of his own. In this way he became a model for later masters of the Edo period in calligraphy as well as in poetry, garden design, and the literati lifestyle.

Jōzan's calligraphy displays refinement, a Sinophile spirit, and a conscious sense of elegance. His range was broad, for he wrote calligraphy in Japanese *kana* and in all five major Chinese script forms. In one long calligraphic hand scroll he wrote out the "Four Admonishments" of Ch'eng Yi (1033–1107) using a different script for each of the four characters of the title (plate 45). Jōzan wrote the four words "See, Hear, Talk, Move" in regular, clerical, running, and cursive scripts, and he used the same sequence of scripts in the smaller calligraphy that follows. In this way he demonstrated his mastery of the Chinese calligraphic tradition, and he began a tradition of alternating scripts within the same scroll that was to become popular among Edo-period calligraphers.

Jōzan is most celebrated for his works in clerical script (Japanese, *reisho*; Chinese, *lishu*). This form of writing was developed by clerks in the Han dynasty (206 B.C.–A.D. 220) as a quicker alternative to the more cumbersome seal script. It was soon supplanted in everyday use, however, by regular, running, and cursive scripts. Clerical script was the first to be written with squared-off linear forms rather than curved lines, and the shape of each character is rectangular or square rather than vertical or rounded. This horizontal structure gives clerical script a sense of formality and repose.

Like the earlier seal script, lines written in clerical script are even rather than modulated, but the significant exception is the *na* stroke, a horizontal movement of the brush which bends diagonally down to the right. The hand pressure is gradually increased as the brush moves to the lowest point, so the line becomes thicker. Then, as the brush moves up to the right, the pressure is released, leaving a triangular shape thinning to a point. The development of the *na* stroke in clerical script is significant as the first instance in Chinese calligraphy that brush lines became strongly modulated, taking advantage of the brush's flexibility. The curving elegance of this stroke is very important to the aesthetics of clerical script, which might otherwise seem excessively even, angular, and square.

Clerical script had been known in Japan before Jōzan's time, but was little used until the seventeenth century. Earlier Japanese commonly wrote in standard, running, and cursive scripts, with an occasional foray into seal script, but clerical script was almost completely ignored. What led Jōzan to use such an obscure script for most of his calligraphy? Upon examination, it can be seen to have a number of features that must have especially appealed to him.

First, clerical script had a flavor of antiquity, since it was associated with the Han dynasty, when it was developed. Jōzan's scholarly persona was based upon the scholar's respect for history and for literature of the past, so this aura of antiquity must have been important to him. Second, clerical script was rarely used in Japan, and therefore could be regarded as a Chinese form of art beyond the norms of ordinary Japanese experience, just like Jōzan's life of retirement in the Shisendō. Third, clerical script required the artist to write each stroke of every character separately, rather than joining them together as in running or cursive scripts. The script emphasized structural elements of design rather than personal exuberance, and it suggested refinement, a quality clearly important to Jōzan. Finally, the decorative formality of clerical script made it suited to signboards and plaques, and Jōzan could utilize it in his calligraphic inscriptions on wooden panels for the Shisendō as well as in scrolls, inscriptions, and albums.

It is not clear which calligrapher was the first to utilize clerical script in the early Edo period. Jōzan seems to have used it the most often, making it a feature of his highly admired calligraphy, but it was also used by a few of his friends. In particular, the master calligrapher Shōkadō Shōjō (c. 1584–1639) occasionally wrote in clerical script in a style rather close to that of Jōzan, even using it at times for his signature on paintings. Shōkadō's death date of 1639 indicates that the advent of the script must have been well before that year, when Jōzan was fifty-six years old. Unfortunately, too few works are dated to establish a chronology; Jōzan tended to add his age on his works only in his final years. In any event, Shōkadō utilized other scripts much more often, while the clerical style was Jōzan's primary script. Thus it seems fair to say that if Jōzan was not the first to use the script in the Edo period, he was certainly the calligrapher who brought it to the fore.

Soon after Jōzan's time, most of the major styles and significant models of Chinese calligraphy were reproduced in woodblock-book form for study in Japan. Jōzan, however, developed his style in clerical script even though he did not have full access to the finest Chinese inscriptions that are now considered the outstanding examples of the script. Jōzan did, however, study a book of Sung-dynasty (960–1279) rubbings called the *Hsing-feng-lou Tieh* published by the scholar Ts'ao Yen-yueh (1157–1228), which reproduced calligraphy by Han-dynasty generals and scholars. Jōzan wrote in a letter to a friend that when he examined the calligraphy of the great military strategist Chu-ko Liang (181–234, page 187), he could understand the transformations of the clerical style—square and round, contracting and expanding—which embrace the spirit manifestations of the Three Spheres (Heaven, Earth, and Man) and encompass the forms of the Eightfold Maze (a pattern of rocks which would conjure up Taoist forces to stymie the enemy). In this way Jōzan expressed his belief in the ability of calligraphy not only to replicate the power of creation but also to influence the world of humans.

Jōzan's calligraphy does emulate the style of the rubbing of Chu-ko Liang in the Sung-dynasty book, although the rubbing itself may represent a later copy of Liang's writing rather than an original work by the general. Han-dynasty inscriptions are considered to be the classical works of clerical script; they usually feature a horizontal thrust in the composition of characters and even straight lines except for the *na* stroke (page 188). Later calligraphy in clerical script tended to become less angular and horizontal, and sometimes to show more modulation of lines. The Han style is generally adhered to in the Chu-ko Liang example that Jōzan admired, but there is more modulation of line, suggesting a date slightly later than the Han dynasty for the brushwork from which first the carving and then the rubbing were made.

Compared with examples of original Han-dynasty script, Jōzan allowed varied line width not only in the *na* stroke, but sometimes in others as well. This may have been due in part to his study of the rubbing of Chu-ko Liang; an "ancient" model would have been extremely important to Jōzan. However, one senses that his well-practiced use of the brush in other scripts had made him comfortable with the effects of varied pressure of the brush. His use of modulated lines produced a modulated effect that is less stringent and more decorative than the classic early models of clerical script.

Jōzan's calligraphy has sometimes been criticized for not following the true ancient style, but in this regard he was certainly a man of his own age. One can see in the calligraphy of Ming (1368–c. 1644) and early Ch'ing-dynasty (c. 1644–1912) masters a similar use of varied lines and elegant compositions; Jōzan must have seen many calligraphic models that are not recorded. In addition, Chinese visitors and immigrants to Japan could have been an important source of inspiration. Jōzan had already developed his style in clerical script before the arrival of Chinese Ōbaku Zen monks after the fall of the Ming dynasty in 1644. Nevertheless, he would most probably have had the opportunity to see the work of immigrant Chinese artists such as the monk Dokuryū (Chinese, Tu-li, 1596–1672), a master calligrapher who came to Japan in 1653. Dokuryū's use of clerical script is surprisingly relaxed and informal (page 189). In his work, the *na* stroke is not emphasized, and the "brushiness" of the calligraphy is deliberately downplayed in favor of modesty and a sense of spaciousness. In comparison, Jōzan's style seems much more studied. He was more interested in the formal and structural properties of the script, which might be called the architectural elements of the calligraphy.

The immigrant Sōtō Zen monk Shin'etsu (Chinese, Hsin-yueh, 1639–96) often utilized clerical script with a more conscious sense of elegance than Dokuryū (page 190). It has sometimes been suggested that Shin'etsu influenced Jōzan, but Jōzan had died by the time Shin'etsu arrived in Japan in 1677, so this was impossible. The important point is that the Chinese artists were utilizing a script that was part of their heritage, while Jōzan was transforming it to suit his own Japanese sense of aesthetics. This cultural difference may help explain the difference in styles, especially the more formally composed writing by Jōzan that suggests he was making a deliberate point of creating a new calligraphic idiom with an antique flavor.

Jōzan probably developed his brushwork style in his early-to-middle years, but he continued to improve his calligraphy over time, as a draft written to the two sons of his friend Hayashi Razan (1583–1657) makes clear (a detail is shown on page 180). This hand scroll, which must be from Jōzan's later years, shows the artist in the activity of creating a long poem in clerical script. From time to time he not only changed his wordings, but occasionally also revised his use of the script itself, writing the same character in a different calligraphic style or making another attempt in the same style. In this draft we can see the mind of Jōzan at work, a rare glimpse into his process of poetic and calligraphic composition. The scroll also demonstrates his mastery of brushwork, making clear that he was exploring the visual effects that he wished to produce. It is also significant that this work was given a laudatory colophon by the major early-nineteenth-century calligrapher, Ichikawa Beian (1779–1858), who also worked extensively in clerical script; Jōzan's influence extended well into the nineteenth century.

One important characteristic of Jōzan's larger-scale calligraphy is his interest in the technique called "flying white," where the paper shows through the brush strokes. This effect is usually created by a brush that is almost dry or that is moved very quickly, or a combination of the two. Clerical script, due to its slow and rather stately pace of execution, does not usually feature "flying white," but it is an integral element of Jōzan's art, perhaps to help mitigate the strong formality of his writing. We may see its full use in most of his larger-scale writing (page 191). At some point in almost all the broad stokes of the brush, the white of the paper shows through.

Because Jōzan's strokes tend to be rather thick and wet, the use of "flying white" give his works a sense of openness and freedom. In examining his works carefully, however, it seems that he did not make this effect by either dry or rapid brushwork but by more deliberate means. He may have especially prepared his brush before each stroke with spaces between the hairs (a technique known as "split brush"), and at times he may also have gone over a single line more than once in order to leave the "flying white" just where he wanted it. Jōzan's calligraphy can be carefully planned, displaying artifice rather than spontaneous freedom of the brush.

Purists might criticize Jōzan for this lack of spontaneity. The question of how Jōzan achieved his "flying white" should, however, be seen in a larger context. Jōzan's simulation of an effect rather than recreation of a process reflects his position in one culture trying to follow the ideals of another. When someone copies a result instead of recreating the impetus that led to the result, something new emerges which must be judged on its own terms. His self-imposed task was to create a personal style within a form of calligraphy that was almost entirely new to Japan while still adhering to Chinese tradition. Jōzan's clerical-script calligraphy has its own sense of beauty, quite unlike anything known before in either China or Japan. His personal combination of elegance, formality, and stately rhythm was perfectly suited to his self-created persona within his self-composed environment. In following the literati ideal, he created unique calligraphy from his own individual interpretation and transformation of the past.

Jōzan may be seen as a forerunner of similar transformations that were to take place when Japanese artists, fascinated with Chinese literati painting, developed their own unique tradition called Nanga. This process might also be compared to the seventeenth-century Italians trying to recreate Greek drama, and in their failure inventing opera. Jōzan accomplished nothing so grand, but he did provide a model for those who wished to adopt a cultivated Chinese lifestyle focused upon the scholarly arts. He also led the way toward the flourishing of *karayō* that lasted for more than three hundred years and is still a feature of Japanese calligraphy today.

In addition to focusing attention on its formal beauty, close examination of Jōzan's calligraphy sheds light on several issues, including that of his personality. Jōzan believed that brushwork expressed the inner character of the artist, writing to a friend that when you look at calligraphy, you see the man. Jōzan, having invented his persona, also endeavored to invent his character in his calligraphy. Theoretically this is impossible, since what the Japanese call "ink traces" are believed to reveal the true nature of the artist no matter what his intention. Nevertheless, there is no doubt that Jōzan did his best to create a persona in his calligraphy as he did in every other aspect of his life. By his decision to create his own style in an ancient and rarely used Chinese script, he gave himself a unique artistic identity, just as he did through the creation of the Shisendō.

Furthermore, in Jōzan's calligraphy, he appears to be consciously rejecting the artistic standards of his era, during which the revival of Heian and

Kamakura styles of *kana* on decorated paper was the outstanding trend. This rejection may be compared to Jōzan's declining a position serving the Tokugawas and his subsequent retirement from all official duties when his mother died. In all cases, he turned against the dominant trends of his era. It appears that in his art as well as in his life, Jōzan deliberately followed his own path. However, we must ask two questions. First, did he truly reject the art of his own time? Second, to what extent does his calligraphy reflect his self-professed values?

During the first decades of the seventeenth century, Japanese calligraphy enjoyed a considerable revival in Kyoto. Masters such as Hon'ami Kōetsu (1558–1637) went far beyond the standards of the late Muromachi period by developing a boldly decorative style in which highly refined technique was put to the service of sumptuous elegance. This style, like that of the newly simplified Zen paintings by Daitokuji monks, was a deliberate revival of the past and therefore a repudiation of trends from more recent centuries. Jōzan's calligraphy certainly does not outwardly resemble the flowing curves of the *kana* scrolls of Kōetsu, but it does consciously revive a past tradition in a very similar way. Furthermore, it shares with Kōetsu's calligraphy a high degree of elaboration leading to an emphasis upon design elements rather than informality and spontaneity. Therefore it is clear that Jōzan accepted one of the underlying tenets of art in his era, the revival of the past, even though he found his models in Chinese rather than Japanese art.

Seen in a broad perspective, the early Edo period artistic revival had historical causes. After more than a century of civil warfare, the new peace and prosperity led to a renewed interest in the arts, with a general rejection of the values of the previous era. For example, in studying the brushwork of the early seventeenth century, it is significant to note that Shōkadō Shōjō did calligraphy in both clerical script and in *kana* on decorated paper, and also painted simplified Zen subjects. These had rather different aesthetic effects; the clerical script was antique and formal, the *kana* was highly decorative, and the painting was informal and sparse. Nevertheless, they all hearkened back to earlier traditions. Jōzan appears more individualistic in his use of clerical script, but his art can be understood as firmly rooted in the underlying aesthetics of his own day.

How much Jōzan's calligraphy reflects his own theories is also an issue that invites our attention. He wrote that he examined and admired rubbings of Han-dynasty calligraphy, but his brushwork reflects the less severe style of Ming-dynasty masters. It seems that this was an artistic choice, just as Jōzan followed trends in Sung and Ming poetry despite his claim that one should follow T'ang masters. We may speculate that Jōzan's theories, in which he felt it vital to stress the past, warred with his own sensibilities, which were (not too surprisingly) those of a man of his own era. By declaring his poetic and calligraphic lineages but not strictly following them, Jōzan invited criticism. In some ways he may have been locked into an untenable situation. He felt it necessary to praise early models in order to establish his independence from the recent past, but in fact he could not avoid being influenced by the creative currents of his own time. Studying both early and later Chinese poetry, he proclaimed the value of the former but was also influenced by the latter; copying models of early and later clerical script, he developed a personal style that owes more to the Ming than the Han aesthetic. More important to the modern viewer, however, are the new elements in his writing that make his calligraphy instantly recognizable. In particular, his large-scale script, with its thick wet lineament and calculated use of "flying white," is unique. Ultimately, Jōzan's image as a lofty recluse was well served by his calligraphy. The elegant formality of his style in a rarely used Chinese script created a cultivated atmosphere of refined beauty, just as he intended.

One way to enjoy the rich ambiguities of Jōzan's art is through his own writings, particularly one significant autobiographical quatrain. He refers to two Chinese precedents. Yuan Ch'ang was an early master of clerical script, while the story of Wheelwright P'ien comes from the third century B.C. Taoist classic *Chuang-tzu*. It seems that P'ien told the Duke of Huan that the books he was reading were nothing but the dregs and leavings of men of old. Angrily questioned by the nobleman, P'ien explained that his own craft as a wheelwright could only be learned through experience. He could understand it in his hands and feel it in his mind, but no words could teach it, nor could it be handed down through books. The Duke was forced to acknowledge this truth. Considering Jōzan's pioneering interest in creatively reviving the Chinese past, his quatrain takes on many levels of meaning:

> In copying clerical characters, I emulated Yuan Ch'ang,
> Reading books, I feel shamed before Wheelwright P'ien.
> Do not be amazed that my frosty whiskers are so long;
> It is due to twisting my beard as I write my poems.

This modest attitude is part of the traditional literati persona, but it also exemplifies Jōzan's spirit. He emulated the ancients as was proper in the scholar-artist tradition, but he never achieved the full naturalness of the adept who does not intellectualize his work. There is a studied quality about Jōzan's writing that is fascinating and frustrating at once—where is the real man underneath? Examining his portrait by the leading painter of his age, Kanō Tan'yū (1602–74), we can see Jōzan as an idealized scholar (page 181). Sitting in Chinese-style raiment and leaning upon an armrest, he gazes off calmly as though he had achieved his ambition as a literatus. The calligraphy Jōzan added above his portrait is elegantly spaced and brushed, and ends with one of his favorite signatures, "Rokurokusanjin," or the Hermit of Six Sixes. Identifying himself with the thirty-six immortal Chinese poets of his choice, Jōzan's created persona was convincing enough to become a model to Japanese literati of the next few centuries.

Some of the most successful calligraphic works of Jōzan exist in the form of signboards and panels. His strong and elegant use of clerical script is ideally suited to carving on boards, and it is one of these wooden panels that first greets the visitor to the Shisendō. Over the second entrance that leads to the villa is a board carved with the words "Plum Gate" (page 191, below). These two characters have been arranged into an elegant geometry that stops just short of rigidity. The word "plum" on the right squeezes the "tree" radical on its left into a tall thin shape, while on the right the shape has been altered into a cross over a large triangle enclosing four smaller triangles. In contrast, the "gate" character on the left has a strong sense of enclosure only alleviated by the bending and slight modulation of the vertical line on the far left that adds a touch of grace to a formal linear structure.

Another calligraphy that was made into an indoor plaque is the single word "Virtue" (page 182). Here the medium is inlaid mother-of-pearl on wood, giving a radiant sparkle to the formal patterning of the brushwork. Jōzan offset the vertical and horizontal structure of his calligraphy here with two modulating diagonal *na* strokes on the left and lower right, adding a sense of movement as well as ultimate balance to the calligraphy. The word "virtue," pronounced *toku* in Japanese, is the first character in the name of the To-kugawa family. Was Jōzan emphasizing his loyalty, or was he merely proclaiming his own sense of virtue?

Jōzan did not only write in clerical script, and some of his other works add significantly to our understanding of his style. A rare single-line calligraphy in cursive script shows his prowess in rapid and dynamic brushwork (page 192). The ink on the brush dried up as it moved down the paper, and the result is a sense of impetuosity and bold confidence. Using only seven strokes to create the four characters within a single gesture, Jōzan filled the space with visual excitement, and he proves that he did not favor clerical script because of any lack of talent in the more informal scripts. What remains similar in all his works is his full utilization of both written areas and negative spaces; we can admire the shapes created where he has *not* written as much as those where he has. Here, for example, in each character there is at least one enclosed area—triangular, oval, or more complex. In the more slowly brushed clerical script, this mastery of negative space is more easily seen (for example in the three small squares in the middle right of "Virtue"), but it is a feature of all of Jōzan's calligraphy.

Jōzan does not seem to have been interested in painting, although he may have brushed an occasional informal work such as a depiction of bamboo, a subject very close in expression to calligraphy. When he wanted portraits of the thirty-six Chinese poets to hang in his villa, he turned to Kanō Tan'yū, the official painter for the Shogunate and a master of Chinese-style art. These imaginary portraits on wood were long hung in the Shisendō, but they are now kept in storage for safekeeping, while copies grace the walls (as on page 184). The originals are now somewhat worn and faded, but they display the elegant styles of both painter and calligrapher (page 183). Tan'yū utilized fine lines of even width for the faces and garments of the Chinese masters, and he enlivened the compositions with quiet but graceful designs on the robes of the poets. His paintings are perfectly matched with Jōzan's restrained calligraphy, which here is modest in size and lineament and calls no attention to itself. When writing out his own poems Jōzan was more assertive, but when he inscribed these portraits he maintained even lines in formal geometric order.

Today visitors can sense the presence of Jōzan throughout the Shisendō, most personally in the calligraphic signboards and scrolls that are everywhere to be seen. It is easy to imagine Jōzan sitting in his Hall of Poetry Immortals, viewing his garden from his elegant villa, surrounded by the portraits of Chinese poets graced by his own inscriptions. Has anyone ever invented such a convincing literati persona?

Jōzan's influence as a calligrapher on later generations was general rather than specific. His world was too self-contained, and no one could convincingly follow him directly. Other masters took up clerical script, but not to the same extent or in the same style as Jōzan. He was primarily revered as a scholar-sage, and his lead was followed in creating a poetic lifestyle more than in the specifics of his art. The Ōbaku Zen monk Monchū (1739–1829), lived two of his final years at the Shisendō; a poem he wrote at the age of ninety is entitled *The Ageless Pine at Shisendō* (page 193). The quatrain in Chinese style could refer equally well to Jōzan, and perhaps it is the kind of epitaph that would most have pleased him:

> When just a few inches tall, where did you come from,
> With your long life of eternal spring?
> The long winds whisper poems endlessly,
> as they shiver your old dragon scales.

The Garden of the Shisendō:
Its *Genius Loci*
Hiroyuki Suzuki

One of the greatest pleasures of visiting Kyoto is viewing its many gardens.

Kyoto's temple complexes each possess lovely gardens in their precincts. Though we may lack the religious impulses our ancestors once felt, paying reverence to the Buddhist images and enjoying the beautiful architecture of these temples still brings us a sense of peace and calm. Kyoto is a contemporary Japanese city. It has many modern buildings, its streets are jammed with traffic, and subways run beneath the ground; yet these temples remain, and their tree-filled precincts cast a green shade that gives Kyoto a unique serenity not seen in other Japanese cities.

How many gardens are there in Kyoto? The large temple complexes contain many smaller subtemples, each possessing its own fine little garden. A subtemple also often possesses a tea room or two, and each tea room has its own small garden. One temple complex may include as many as thirty distinct gardens. The traditional-style homes of Kyoto, the *machiya,* also always include two or three miniature gardens. These "courtyard" gardens are not visible to people walking on the street; no sign even hints at their presence. They can only be seen when you are invited into the home and led back to the drawing room, which usually opens out onto an inner garden.

Private gardens lie hidden away in the recesses of homes on Kyoto's busiest, most bustling streets. The existence of these invisible gardens lends the city a stillness, an indescribable depth. Visitors from afar walk the city's streets aware of these countless unseen gardens, and their invisible presence lends the city a rare charm.

Of course the gardens inside Kyoto's *machiya* are small—the smallest may be no more than a meter on a side. In that tiny space, a miniature garden is created from simple elements—a charming little tree; a stone washbasin; a carpet of moss. A special feature of the Japanese garden art is the attention paid to creating a feeling of spaciousness greater than the actual area available.

The poet Saisei Murō (1889–1962), a great admirer of gardens and a hobbyist gardener himself, wrote about the gardens in Kyoto's *machiya*.

> It would appear that there are many of those small gardens, so beautifully made, among the houses and gardens in the middle of the city; yet I was not able to see even one of them. They possess a significance quite different from the famous public garden spaces; among them are many charming spots in which I would like to live, to breathe, myself. The mornings were always cloudy, and the light cast by the sun, weak and cold, seemed without brightness and lacking any direction. Whatever garden I saw or walked about in, I found moss growing, and those sunken colors blended perfectly in the shade. This atmosphere, this wetness, it seemed to me, had, together with the lackluster light, helped create just the kind of gardens so characteristic of Kyoto.[1]

Gardens that a traveler cannot see are private gardens. And precisely because they are private, they have such a strong allure. The garden of the Shisendō is not a courtyard garden in the city, but it is private. It is far more spacious than an urban garden and, surrounded as it is by the rural scenery of the outskirts of Kyoto, it has an entirely different feeling; but as a garden created for its owner's personal enjoyment it has something in common with the courtyard gardens of Kyoto homes. This is not a formal resemblance so much as a similarity in our response when we experience the garden.

Shisendō lies tucked away on the city's outskirts. It is a private mountain villa. Today it is open to the public, and tourists and travelers are free to visit it, but originally the buildings and gardens were accessible only to their owner, the poet Ishikawa Jōzan, and his intimate friends. When we visit Shisendō today, we should do so as if we were Jōzan's guests, too.

1. Murō Saisei, "Nihon no Niwa," in *Asahi Shimbun, Asahi Shinsensho* 10, 1943, 262.

Jōzan owned a large amount of property in this area, nestled in the mountains that surround the basin in which Kyoto lies. Documents concerning the disposition of the property after his death show that the upper residence occupied 579 *tsubo* (1,930 square meters) and the lower residence 380 *tsubo* (1,254 square meters). In addition, cultivated fields and part of the facing mountainside were included in the property. The fields attached to it provided the poet Jōzan an independent living during his retirement in the midst of nature. Today, approximately 680 *tsubo* (2,233 square meters) of the Shisendō property have been designated a historical landmark, and another 1,000 *tsubo* (3,333 square meters) occupied by farmland and buildings are attached to the Shisendō.

Spacious as the site might be, the Shisendō was built as a place for a poet to live in quiet retirement from the city. There was no need to construct a grand edifice or splendid garden, and both buildings and garden are on a small scale. The ideal of the Japanese poet was to live in serene solitude in the countryside, enjoying the beauties of nature. Jōzan's particular ideal was to create, in a variety of forms, a mutual rapport between his poetry and the natural setting that was his home. Jōzan was born in 1583 and died in 1672, placing him a century before the English poet Alexander Pope (1688–1744), who advocated many of the same values.

In his own context, Jōzan's ideals were not unique. They were shared by many Japanese poets in his day, who glorified nature in their poetry and at the same time apprehended the world of nature through the poetic medium. As a result, the gardens they created were not merely compositions of natural elements simply arranged and beautifully ordered; instead, they sought to express meaning through poetic symbols. Only when poetry and garden were taken together could their true significance be appreciated. This conception of life was the ideal of the poets of the time, who were known as literati, or *bunjin*.

The name Shisendō, or Hall of the Poetry Immortals, refers to Jōzan's selection of thirty-six famous Chinese poets as symbols of his hermitage, which he decorated with their portraits. The number thirty-six has a long tradition in Japan. Thirty-six masters of the classical, thirty-one-syllable po-

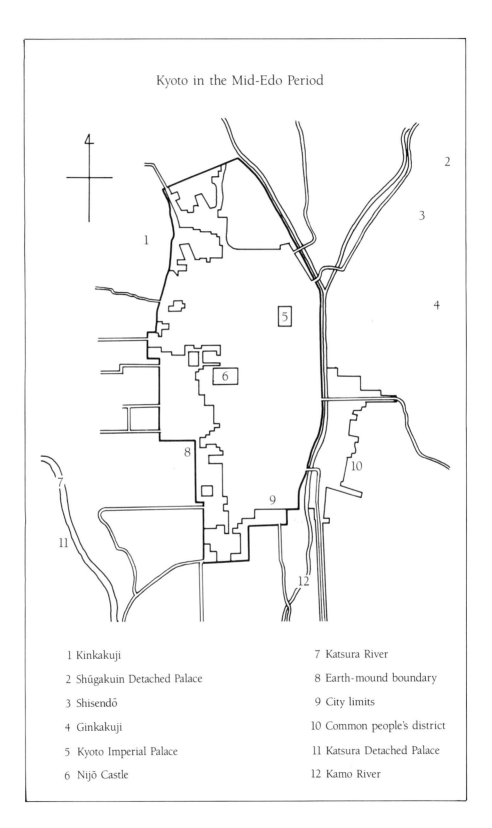

Kyoto in the Mid-Edo Period

1 Kinkakuji

2 Shūgakuin Detached Palace

3 Shisendō

4 Ginkakuji

5 Kyoto Imperial Palace

6 Nijō Castle

7 Katsura River

8 Earth-mound boundary

9 City limits

10 Common people's district

11 Katsura Detached Palace

12 Kamo River

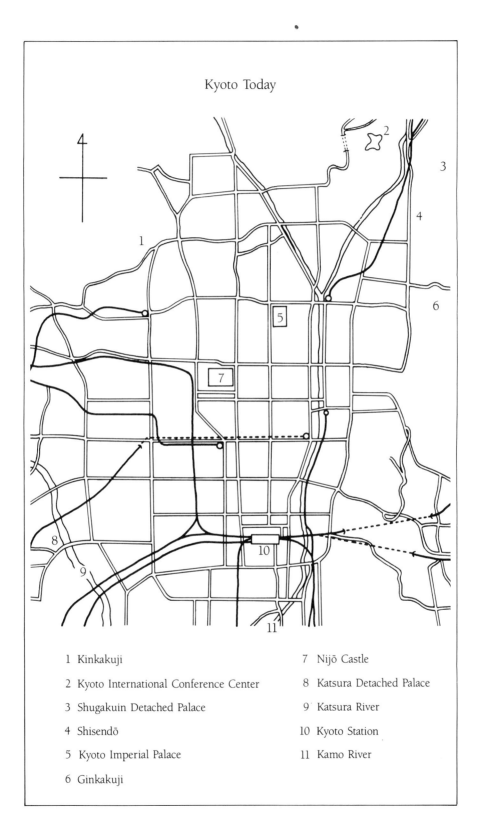

Kyoto Today

1 Kinkakuji

2 Kyoto International Conference Center

3 Shugakuin Detached Palace

4 Shisendō

5 Kyoto Imperial Palace

6 Ginkakuji

7 Nijō Castle

8 Katsura Detached Palace

9 Katsura River

10 Kyoto Station

11 Kamo River

etic form known as *waka* poetry were selected and dubbed the thirty-six "immortals of *waka*" (*kasen*). Jōzan's selections were masters of classical Chinese poetry (*shi*), so they became the *shisen*. *Dō* means "hall." Jōzan's merging of Chinese and Japanese poetic traditions is apparent not only in his intellectual and artistic life but in the way he designed his garden as well. In spite of the alterations and additions to the structures and the garden of the Shisendō, we can still sense Jōzan's intent when we visit this quiet Kyoto suburb today.

The Shisendō is located in an area of the city now famous for a number of beautiful gardens and teahouses constructed during the Edo period, among them the Shūgakuin and the Manshūin. Near Jōzan's villa, in the area known as Kudarimatsu (Descending Pine), one must climb upwards along a narrow road to reach the gate of Jōzan's retreat. The small size of the gate surprises many visitors. The spot gives a sense of being altogether deserted. Though at first glance the gate seems ordinary, as if it might be the entrance to anyone's property, it is the entrance to Jōzan's distinctive world. As we enter the gate and climb the stone steps, we arrive at a second, inner gate, also small. On either side of the stone steps are groves of bamboo. The narrow path linking the two gates accentuates the beauty of the bamboo, changing from season to season.

After passing through the second gate, the Shisendō complex comes into view. The eye is caught at once by the small curved windows, in the Chinese style, cut in the wall. There is a real sense of entering a special environment.

Stepping up to the building, it is clear at once that the garden can be experienced from every room. At a glance we intuit that the whole environment has been conceived to merge the buildings with their natural setting. Passing through the Hall of the Poetry Immortals, where the Chinese poets' portraits hang, we arrive immediately at the southwest room, also constructed during Jōzan's time, which opens beautifully onto the garden space. Looking out toward the garden, the tiny rivulet called by Jōzan the Shallow of Floating Leaves is visible on the left. This area just in front of the Hall of the Poetry Immortals is a vestige of how the garden must have looked originally. During Jōzan's time the garden probably had a more hushed, an emptier atmosphere than it does today.

The modern garden, to the south where the earth slopes downwards, is charming as well. In a spot where a waterfall slips down the hill, a hedge of pruned azaleas has been created, and in front of it stands a large, solitary red pine. On the near side of the green border, the pine branches hang down toward the south, so that the distant scenery can be observed through its delicate needles.

THE GARDEN OF THE SHISENDŌ, looking south from the main reception room of the complex. The curving hedge boundary along the western edge and the straight boundary along the east closely reflect the original site. Vegetable gardens were planted in the open space outside the hedge on the west, and the area in front of the Nest For Hunting Among the Rue was once a flower bed. The gates and stone steps leading up to the Shisendō and several important features of the site are to the north, on the opposite side of the complex (see the map on page 105).

Descending further down into the lower garden, one notices over on the eastern side, near a small garden pavilion, the tiny Waterfall for Washing Away Ignorance. Although very small, the flow sends up a delicate splash when it strikes the rock—a scene that Jōzan described as "The Waterfall Down the Cliff Wall." Passing by the waterfall, then taking the path by the small building, one suddenly catches a glimpse of the Tower for Whistling at the Moon, with its unusual, projecting architecture. It is completely asymmetrical, and with its roofing partly of tile and partly of straw, which harmonize so well, it creates a truly astonishing effect. When one takes into account that the rooms to the eastern side of the Hall of the Poetry Immortals were added later, the building must have appeared all the more eccentric when it was first constructed.

The Shisendō as it survives today is quite different from what it was during Jōzan's lifetime. The central Hall of the Poetry Immortals and the adjoining Tower for Whistling at the Moon are original structures, and there were once other rooms adjoining these, different in arrangement than they are today. Japanese wooden architecture can easily be dismantled and rearranged, and changes of this sort are a frequent occurrence.

To the literati of Jōzan's age, the study (shosai) was the most important room of their residence. It was there that they composed poetry and communed with nature. The Hall of the Poetry Immortals is the study of the Shisendō. Commonly, a room for tea-drinking was situated next to the study. This was not necessarily a formal Japanese-style tea-ceremony room; the literati regarded tea drinking as important because it was a custom said to have been favored by Chinese poets of old.

Another small room was typically built for enjoying the garden, a room similar in function to the English folly—a small, picturesque pavilion or summerhouse, often of fanciful design. At the Shisendō, this is the Tower for Whistling at the Moon. In the garden, flowing water and flowers were desirable features. The interest in flowers derived again from Chinese poets, who enjoyed discussing the merits of various flowers and arguing which was superior.

The tradition of literati tastes lives in the Shisendō. The literati preferred informal styles over formal, and aimed to create a spontaneous, natural appearance—though in fact great pains were taken to achieve this. This style of architecture is called *sukiya* architecture.

Sukiya, which might be translated as "pavilion of elegant curiosities," contrasts with the more formal architectural model known as the *shoin,* or "study for writing." These two distinct styles became the prototypes for the residences of those with an interest in literary pursuits, and those of means and culture, during this period. To understand traditional Japanese architecture it is essential to grasp the distinction between these two basic styles.

The main elements of a room in the formal *shoin* style were the traditional ornamental alcove, the tokonoma; a desk, usually at right angles to the tokonoma, set into a small bay window to allow light to enter (the *tsukeshoin*); and staggered display shelves (*chigaidana*). The tokonoma was decorated with a hanging scroll, flowers, and small decorative objects. The staggered display shelves were located next to the tokonoma and also provided storage space for small objects. The sliding wooden doors of the room (*fusuma*) were decorated with paintings, and crossbars called *nageshi* were placed at the upper edges of the sliding door frames to support them. The *nageshi* were held in place with nails, and the nail heads were covered with decorative hardware. All of the timber used in the *shoin* was planed square and smooth to reveal the wood grain.

The *sukiya* style, however, was designed to provide more intimate enjoyment. Elements such as a tokonoma, shelves, and *tsukeshoin* could be employed, but the wood used to construct them was as thin as possible, to create a delicate feeling, and idiosyncratic decorative motifs created a diverting atmosphere. The sliding wooden doors were not decorated with elaborate formal paintings. If art work was desired, lightly sketched pictures or abstract design patterns were preferred. Long horizontal strips of wood at the tops of the sliding panels were generally not employed; they tended to enhance the horizontality of the room, making the atmosphere heavier. On those rare occasions when they were used with the *sukiya* style, the bark was left on the thin logs that were chosen. Sometimes the walls and pillars were colored, and the pillars were most frequently made of natural, unplaned wood. All of these techniques created an atmosphere in which the viewer felt close to nature.

The Shisendō shows elements of the *sukiya* style, which was considered appropriate for a *bunjin* living in retreat in the countryside. Perhaps the most striking element in the building is the two-story Tower for Whistling at the Moon. The tower and the room with the portraits of the thirty-six poets make up the original center of a complex of rooms. The unusually constructed tower provides the real focal point of the entire structure and strongly suggests the mood of *sukiya* style.

Two-story structures were seldom built in Japan. There are many examples of five-story pagodas and two-story gates, but they were not usually functional—they were designed to be viewed from the outside rather than climbed up inside. The quarters of the head monk of some Zen temples, however, were two stories high. At Kenchōji in Kamakura, for example, there was a two-story structure called the Togetsurō (Tower for Winning the Moon), and at Kenninji in Kyoto there was a similar structure called Jishikaku (The Pavilion of the Compassionate Gaze). In present-day Kyoto, two famous structures, the Golden Pavilion and the Silver Pavilion, are rare surviving examples of medieval two-story structures.

In two-story structures that were part of Zen-temple complexes, the upper stories were constructed so that one could actually climb to the second story and look out from there. This was not an architecture to be looked at but one to be used for looking. The main gates of Zen temples were designed with Buddhist images (usually the sixteen arhats) placed on the second story, and people could climb up to view them. The Chinese two-story gates and towers, which provided the models for Japanese temple architecture, were designed so that people could climb to the second floor. Non-functional two-story structures were a peculiarly Japanese development. The original Chinese tradition is reflected in the functional two-story Zen-temple architecture that was newly imported from China during the medieval period.

Zen temples often also included structures built on the peaks of hills that were called *azumaya,* intended to provide an opportunity to enjoy looking out over the landscape. Musō Sōseki (1275–1351), the famed Zen priest and landscape gardener, is said to have constructed such a small pavilion that he named Sekai Ichiran Tei, The Pavilion of the Whole World at a Single Glance. At the famous Saihōji ("Moss Temple") in the southwestern suburbs of Kyoto, a small pavilion was built that commands a fine view. It is named the Shukuentei, Pavilion to Seize the Far-Distant View. As their names show, these structures were constructed in places where the view could be enjoyed.

Pleasure at viewing the scenery from a second story became, in the later Tokugawa period, an important factor in *sukiya* architecture, which became increasingly popular. Perhaps the best surviving example from this period in Kyoto is the Hiunkaku (Pavilion of the Flying Clouds), located in the Nishi Honganji temple complex. Records indicate that in 1709, a two-story building was constructed in the palace built for Emperor Higashiyama's (r. 1687–1709) retirement. A pictorial map of the period also reveals that a two-story structure was constructed at the residence of the Konoe family. In the 1660s, a two-story pavilion was constructed at the residence of the retired emperor Gomizunoo (r. 1611–29). When Ishikawa Jōzan constructed his Shisendō in l641, it is likely that there was already a small number of structures similar to the Tower for Whistling at the Moon in existence. The custom of climbing to the upper story to eat and drink, or to write Chinese or Japanese poems, was already becoming established, and with it the second story evolved from the decorative to the functional.

The *shoin* and earlier Japanese architectural styles were largely symmetrical in layout and form. The new *sukiya* architecture was asymmetrical, presenting a shape as curious and intriguing as possible. The tiny, second-story space at the Shisendō, for example, perches on the roof in a way that destroys all ordinary sense of proportion, making the large round window overlooking the garden appear all the more eccentric.

The *sukiya* style shuns orthodoxy; it is purposely lighthearted and self-consciously quaint—perfectly suited, it turns out, to men who had rejected cultural orthodoxy and left behind the ways of the world.

The documents concerning the Shisendō that date from the time of Jōzan suggest that the Tower for Whistling at the Moon jutted out so that those seated in the tower must have felt right in the midst of the garden. To look down at the garden was one way of enjoying it, and the second-story room must have been one means for Jōzan to entertain his visitors. *A Record of the Shisendō,* written in 1643 by Jōzan's friend Hayashi Razan (1583–1657), makes this function clear: "At that point, I entered into this tiny building, crossed through the study, then immediately climbed to the Tower for Whistling at the Moon." Jōzan took Razan to the tower as soon as he had welcomed him to the villa. From there both could observe the distant streets of the capital and admire the beauties of nature that surrounded them. At a time when such structures were still comparatively rare, this was an unusual and valuable opportunity and must have provided great pleasure for Jōzan's visitors.

The official visit by Emperor Gomizunoo in 1626 to the shogun, Tokugawa Iemitsu (1604–51), at Nijō castle in Kyoto provides an example of the novelty and interest of second-story views at the time. During his tour of the castle, the emperor stated that he would very much enjoy climbing the Tenshūkaku (The Tower of Heavenly Protection), and he mounted to the very top. The structure, built atop a stone wall fifteen meters high, rose up another twenty-seven meters. The view must have been truly superb. The shogun's original itinerary had not included a visit by the emperor to the top of the tower, and the shogun and his retinue were surprised at this sudden request. During the five days of his visit, the Emperor climbed to the top twice to amuse himself with the view.

This episode shows how few buildings of this sort had been constructed and how rare were the occasions when they could be entered. What pleasure visitors to the Shisendō must have taken at this opportunity—and at such a distance from the city itself.

What form did the gardens at the Shisendō take?

Though they have been much altered since Jōzan's time, something of his real intentions surely remains even today, and with the help of surviving documents it is possible to visualize the original gardens.

Within the garden, Jōzan identified ten "locales" and twelve "scenes." This was a pleasant device that many cultivated people in the Tokugawa period enjoyed.

The origin of this concept was the Chinese tradition of the famous Eight

Views of the Hsiao and Hsiang Rivers. In the Northern Sung Dynasty (960–1126) the painter Sung Ti (fl. eleventh century) chose eight scenes to paint in the area of Hunan Province, which became known as the Eight Views of Hsiao and Hsiang. Since that time, other painters took up the same themes countless times. These Eight Views were:

1. View of clear-weather mists above a mountain market-village
2. View of a fishing village at sunset
3. View of a sailboat returning to a distant inlet
4. View of the confluence of the Hsiao and Hsiang rivers in the rain
5. View of a temple bell in the evening mist
6. View of the autumn moon over Tung-t'ing Lake
7. View of geese descending to a sandbar
8. View of snow falling on a river at dusk[2]

These Eight Views became widely popular; in Japan as well, painters and poets took up these themes in their work.

Eventually, a similar group of eight views was chosen from the area surrounding Lake Biwa, Japan's largest interior body of water, which is located near Kyoto. These eight views came to be called The Eight Views of Ōmi, since Lake Biwa is situated in the area traditionally referred to as Ōmi.

1. View of the town of Awazu on a clear and windy day
2. View of the village of Seta at sunset
3. View of a sailboat returning off the shore of Yabashi
4. View of Karasaki in the night rain
5. View of the evening bell at Mii temple near Lake Biwa
6. View of the autumn moon over Ishiyama temple near Lake Biwa
7. View of geese landing near Katada
8. View of snow falling at dusk from Mount Hira, overlooking Lake Biwa[3]

2. The Chinese readings for these eight views are: (1) *shan-shih ch'ing-lan*; (2) *yü-ts'un hsi-chao*; (3) *yuan-p'u kuei-fan*; (4) Hsiao Hsiang *yeh-yü*; (5) *yen-ssu wan-chung*; (6) Tung-t'ing *ch'iu-yueh*; (7) *p'ing-sha lo-yen*; and (8) *chiang-t'ien mu-hsueh*.

3. The Eight Views of Ōmi in Japanese are: (1) Awazu *no seiran*; (2) Seta *no yūshō*; (3) Yabashi *kihan*; (4) Karasaki *yau*; (5) Mii *no banshō*; (6) Ishiyama *shūgetsu*; (7)Katada *no rakugan*; and (8) Hira *no bosetsu*.

A comparison of the Eight Views of Hsiao and Hsiang with the Eight Views of Ōmi shows that the subject matter of these two sets is exactly the same. Both depict windy days, sunsets, returning sailboats, rainy nights, evening temple bells, autumn moons, geese landing on sandbars, and evening snows. The only difference is that the location has shifted from China to Japan.

My point is not that the Japanese are skilled at copying. Rather, I wish to consider why the Japanese took an interest in the Eight Views and why it later became the vogue in Japan to select these eight views to paint.

After the Eight Views of Ōmi, there were the Eight Views of Kyoto, Eight Views of the Southern Capital (that is, Nara), Eight Views of Sen'yūji Temple (in Kyoto), Eight Views of Azuma (another name for Edo), Eight Views of Fukagawa (an area of Edo)—the list is long. Japanese artists found eight places to paint inside a city, a district, a compound, the precincts of a temple or shrine, sometimes even in a single building. During the Edo period it was fashionable to select eight views inside the gardens of the feudal lords. For instance, there were eight views in the Rikugien garden at Komagome and of the Yūin'en garden in Ichigaya, both in Edo.

Even after Japan began to modernize in the Meiji period, this notion of eight views persisted. In 1928, for example, the *Mainichi Shimbun* of Osaka and the *Nichi-Nichi Shimbun* of Tokyo, with support from the Ministry of Railroads, selected Eight Views of Japan and published a travel guide about them. In 1932, the *Hōchi Shimbun* commemorated its twenty thousandth issue and Tokyo's establishment of thirty-five municipal wards by selecting Eight Newly Chosen Places in Tokyo and erecting monuments at each of the chosen sites. The famous novelist Dazai Osamu (1901–48) wrote a short novel in 1941 entitled *Eight Views of Tokyo,* knowing that his readers would grasp the allusion at once. This literary and spatial concept of eight views has continued to appeal to the Japanese from the medieval period to the modern era.

One Japanese-language dictionary explains the meaning of eight views (*hakkei*) as "a collection of eight scenes, selected from within a given space, that are admired for their beauty." Yet as we have already seen, the concept of eight views also involves the selection of certain conditions—such as the season, time of day, and weather—that suit a given space, and represents an

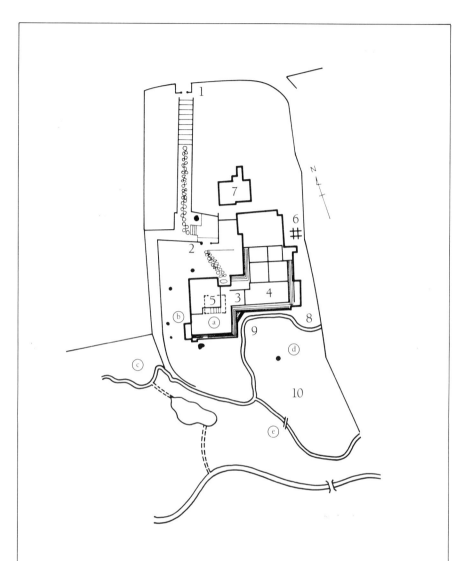

THE TEN LOCALES OF THE ŌTOTSUSŌ, the proper name for the complex we commonly call the Shisendō, are: (1) Lesser Paradise-Cave. (2) Old Plum Gate. (3) Hall of the Poetry Immortals. (4) Nest for Hunting Among the Rue. (5) Tower for Whistling at Moon. (6) Spring of the Vital Region. (7) Pavilion of Leaping from the Deep. (8) Waterfall for Washing Away Ignorance. (9) Shallow of Floating Leaves. (10) Embankment of a Hundred Flowers.

The large room south of the Tower and the Hall is the main reception room (a). Next to it on the left is the privy (b). Beyond the hedge boundary of the upper garden is the garden pavilion called the Pavilion of the Waning Moon (*Zangetsuken*, c) and the small pagoda (d) and "deer-scarer" water mortar (e) are located in the garden south of the Nest for Hunting Among the Rue.

attempt to capture the exquisite nature of that combination. A beautiful place is not to be measured simply in terms spatial design but in terms of the design of space-time.

Japanese culture puts a high value on phenomena that are a fusion of time and space. The element of time is always incorporated into space in the design process. The significance of space is affected by temporal changes, and the Japanese seek to appreciate space at the best moment—whether a season, like autumn, or a time of day, like sunset.

Ishikawa Jōzan's choice of his ten locales and twelve scenes owes a great deal to his awareness of the eight scenes derived from Chinese sources. But the number of scenes was not limited to eight; there are examples of ten, twelve, and even groups extending to a hundred. In China during the same Northern Sung period, a selection of the Ten Scenes of the West Lake was already well known, and during the Southern Sung Period (1127–1279), the painter Hsia Kuei (active first half of the thirteenth century) had already produced his series Twelve Scenes of Hills and Waters.

It is not surprising that Jōzan, who felt such a deep affinity for Chinese culture, should emulate scenes so appreciated by poets and painters alike. His choice of twelve rather than eight scenes may well reflect the fact that the Chinese-inspired eight scenes had already become so popular in Japan that he felt that they had lost their uniquely Chinese flavor. Jōzan had taken the tradition of thirty-six *waka* poets and transposed it to China in selecting his thirty-six poetry immortals; why not extend the traditional Chinese views to twelve? Jōzan recast a Japanese cultural concept into Chinese terms and a Chinese concept into the cultural context of a Japanese garden with considerable sophistication.

With this background, let us now look at the specific locales and scenes chosen for the Shisendō. The ten locales of the Shisendō are:

1. Lesser Paradise Cave (the small gate at the entrance to the Shisendō)
2. Old Plum Gate (the second gateway at the top of the stone stairs)
3. Hall of the Poetry Immortals (the room in which hang the portraits of the thirty-six Chinese poets chosen by Jōzan)

4. Nest for Hunting Among the Rue (a small room for reading)

5. Tower for Whistling at Moon (the small room on the second floor constructed for viewing the landscape)

6. Spring of the Vital Region (a deep well near the room set aside for reading)

7. Pavilion of Leaping from the Deep (a room for servants who assisted in the villa)

8. Waterfall for Washing Away Ignorance (a small waterfall in the garden)

9. Shallow of Floating Leaves (a tiny stream of water flowing from the waterfall)

10. Embankment of a Hundred Flowers (a slope planted with flowers near the waterfall)[4]

Jōzan named these the ten locales of the Ōtotsusō [Trompe L'oeil Nest],[5] a name which, strictly speaking, is the correct one to refer to the house and grounds as they stand now. Shisendō (the third locale above) is only one of the ten locales, one element of the Ōtotsusō.

Jōzan clearly took great pains to include among the ten locales several that Chinese *bunjin* traditionally considered ideal rustic environments. In particular the study, the tower for viewing the landscape, and the waterfall with its flowing current, as well as the slope of flowers in bloom.

A device called a *sōzu,* usually translated as "water mortar" or "deer-scarer," is installed in one corner of the garden. This is a closed bamboo tube through which water flows; when the tube is filled, it tips of its own weight. The water spills out when the tube strikes a stone installed below the pivot on which it moves. The high, clear sound created reverberates throughout the garden. Originally such a sound was intended to chase away sparrows, wild boars, or

4. In Japanese, the ten locales are: (1) Shōyūdō; (2) Rōbaikan; (3) Shisendō; (4) Ryōgeisō; (5) Shōgetsurō; (6) Kōkōsen; (7) Yakuenken; (8) Semmōbaku; (9) Ryūyōhaku; and (10) Hyakkanō.
5. Jōzan doubtless borrowed this term from traditions surrounding the work of the Chinese painter Chang Seng-yu (active 500–550), who was known for his renderings of landscapes and Buddhist and Taoist figures. At the Temple of the Single Vehicle in Nanking, he is said to have painted pictures in a "concave-convex" style (*yao-tieh* in Chinese, *ōtotsu* in Japanese) which appeared three-dimensional, i.e., trompe l'oeil.

deer that might harm the flowers or crops. It is said that the device was first created by farmers to protect the fields they tilled in mountain areas, which is doubtless why Jōzan installed the device in his garden. In Jōzan's time, deer and wild boar might still have disturbed the garden, but it is more likely that the *sōzu* was installed to intensify the effect of the surrounding silence. Its sharp, resonant sound reinforces the listener's presence at the base of a mountain, far from the noisy turmoil of the city. Jōzan may have been the first to install a *sōzu* in a garden; afterward the *sōzu* became used more and more frequently in a variety of settings as a favorite means to produce a sense of quiet.

The ten locales and the *sōzu* that Jōzan installed in his garden show us what elements defined the Shisendō as an appropriately isolated place for a *bunjin* to live. What idea did the twelve scenes represent, then? Let us examine them one by one:

1. Cherry Blossoms Filling the Path (a small cherry tree with profuse blossoms on the small path running along the valley in the garden)
2. Plowing in the Rain at the Village Out Front (the sight of the farmer in the neighboring village plowing his fields in the rain)
3. The Waterfall Down the Cliff Wall (the sound of the water of the cascade to wash away ignorance, as it splashes on the rocks)
4. The Moon's Reflection in the Stepping-stone Pond (the sight of the moon reflected on the surface of the pond in the garden)
5. Red Leaves Along the Stream (colored leaves near a stream coming from the mountain)
6. Snow Piled High on Mountains All Around (snow on the peaks of the four surrounding mountains)
7. Leisurely Clouds Above the Peak of Mount T'ai (peaceful clouds that can be seen far off at the top of Mount Hiei, to the north of Kyoto)
8. The Long Flow of the Kamo River (the leisurely flow of the Kamo river, far to the west)
9. Evening Mist over the Capital (smoke from the cooking of the evening meal rising from Kyoto)

10. The City Walls of Osaka (the sight of Osaka castle, dimly made out far in the distance)

11. The Sound of the Pines from Beyond the Garden (echoes of the wind in the pines planted outside the garden)

12. The Shrine in the Woods at the Neighboring Hamlet (a small shrine amidst the trees in a neighboring village)[6]

Ishikawa Jōzan had a picture scroll of these scenes prepared, which he titled *A Pictorial Record of Twelve Scenes at the Ōtotsusō,* and he wrote a number of poems to accompany them. Jōzan's twelve scenes functioned much like the Sung-dynasty Eight Views of Hsiao and Hsiang, or the Japanese Eight Scenes of Ōmi. Some of the sites Jōzan selected could not, however, be observed from the Shisendō. It was impossible to glimpse the outlines of Osaka castle from Kyoto, and it is unlikely that the Kamo River could have been seen from the villa, either. And since the Shisendō was constructed in the foothills of a mountain, Mount Hiei could not have been visible from the garden.

In sum, these twelve scenes which extend the Shisendō beyond the villa proper were chosen to stimulate the imagination; they are an aesthetic method. Each includes some aspect that cannot be seen from the villa itself, yet because each puts the poetic imagination to work, all of the natural beauties of Kyoto that surrounded the villa were brought into Jōzan's environment. With the twelve scenes, Jōzan introduced a vast expanse into this little country house. The scenes also included distinctive time elements—spring and fall scenery, the mood of dusk, a rainy, cloudy, or windy day—so that expanses of both time and space were incorporated into the world of the Shisendō.

Though they were not actually visible, Jōzan included famous places and buildings that surrounded the Shisendō—sites rich in historical and cultural associations such as Osaka Castle, the Kamo River, and Mount Hiei. Because these places were so famous as the stage for many important historical events,

---

6. In Japanese, the twelve scenes are: (1) *man kei ōka;* (2) *zen son ri u;* (3) *gan sho baku sen;* (4) *sei chi in getsu;* (5) *keihen kōyō;* (6) *shizan kō setsu;* (7) *tai kyō kan un;* (8) Kōga *chōryū;* (9) Rakuyō *ban en;* (10) *nan ba jō yō;* (11) *en gai shō sei;* and (12) *rin kyoku sō shi.*

their very names aroused a wealth of associations. Jōzan used these associations to make the world surrounding the Shisendō even richer and more evocative.

The Shisendō is no more than a tiny villa in the foothills of the mountains at Kyoto's edge. But by selecting these twelve scenes, with a single gesture Jōzan provided his villa great expanse and resonance in both time and space. He did not flee the bustle of the city and set up house alone in the mountains because he sought a realm of primitive isolation. The world of the Shisendō is a world firmly linked to the cultural tradition, yet free from the noise and bother of city life. This was Jōzan's ideal. The act of choosing twelve scenes was a means of linking, through the power of association, his life of retreat in the mountains to the cultural tradition, and extending that life into the flow of nature and history. This was the *bunjin*'s ideal, and the Shisendō's essence.

(translated by J. Thomas Rimer)

The Hall of the Poetry Immortals
Shūichi Katō

It was April when I made a solitary visit to the Shisendō. It's not as if I set out to visit the place, but somehow I found myself forced away from the noise and bustle of Kyoto and on my way to that quiet northeast corner of the city.

Generally, I am not fond of visiting famous sites and hallowed ruins. I know that today, when a modern superhighway speeds through the heart of old Nihombashi, pilgrimages to famous sites of old are bound to be fraught with disappointment and regrets for their disappearance. Of course the ancient Buddhist temples and Shinto shrines still survive in Kyoto. They beg for our contributions in their offering boxes, and in return they show their stuff; they might call the fee they charge an offering, but it's really nothing more than a sight-seeing charge. And that pretense is precisely what I dislike about the tourist enterprises of temples and shrines, and why I always avoid them. Well, if not always, at least in April, when I stay away from the famous temples of Kyoto. The dust raised by cars and buses of tourists, a new one arriving on the heels of each that departs, darkens the sky and I watch the familiar rooftops from afar as they appear and fade again through the clouds of grime.

"Shisendō?" Where are you from?" she asked.

The girl I queried at Shūgakuin didn't know the Shisendō. But I had been there before. I'd probably remember the way as I walked in that direction. As you near the Shisendō, the path among the trees rises suddenly and sharply. I took off my jacket; the cool air on my damp skin felt good. The white sand of the path, the smell of the farmer's plots that drifted into the cedar grove—sensations of a world that I had long forgotten. Shisendō's unassuming outer gate stood quietly before me.

The garden was quiet, too.

Entering the outer gate, you follow a path of stepping stones and are soon at the entrance to the site. The building is simple, with no marked artistry. The front and right sides of the relatively large main room open to the garden, and on the left are a study, a tea room, and a kitchen. In the study, poems of the great Chinese masters of poetry are displayed, copied in the ancient calligraphic style for which the master of the Shisendō was renowned. This, of course, is the origin of the name Shisendō, the Hall of Poetry Immortals. Every room allows access to the garden, which is small—you can easily see the whole thing in less than ten minutes, yet it contains a stream splashing against stones, a narrow path with all sorts of unexpected twists and turns, rock formations that suddenly appear before you, and a grove of trees, dense, sparse, and dense again, leading to a valley. A formidable artistry was needed to incorporate so many changes and devices in such a limited space and yet avoid a feeling of overcrowding. I could care less about the twelve scenes and ten locales that the garden is famous for. As I said earlier, I'm not much interested in famous sights. Still, however little I may care for such things, it is impossible to pass by, for example, Ama no Hashidate at Katsura Detached Palace without at least taking note of its existence. But you can easily pass by the twelve scenes and ten locales of the Shisendō, even if you know them well. The designer of this garden had no intention of cluttering it with sights that, even in as ample a garden as that of Katsura Detached Palace, are an irritating intrusion. In fact, in one sense this garden is quite spacious. The wooded valley leads right into the forests that drape the slopes of Higashiyama. This is not the well-known device of the Japanese garden art called "borrowed landscapes"; it's just that the garden has no clear boundary. With the broad expanse of the spring sky open above and the sun pouring down on the garden below, the garden looks like a pleasant and sunny spot you just happened upon on the mountainside. Two boys and a girl, apparently students, were strolling slowly in that sunlight. From time to time the call of a bush warbler echoed from the direction of the valley stream. A line from a poem by the master of this house drifted into my thoughts.

At the deserted cloister, not a soul.
Noontime in spring, eternity.

That master was Ishikawa Jōzan. According to the chronology put together by

Hitomi Chikudo, Jōzan quit his post as a samurai and retired to this spot in 1640, when he was fifty-eight. For more than thirty years, until his death at ninety, he closed his gates and declined visits, and though he "viewed the hearth smoke of the capital at dusk," he never crossed the Kamo River again. "By nature he loved cleanliness, and he often picked up the broom to sweep the garden himself," so that not one speck of dust remained. From this casual remark in the biographer's account, I imagined the relationship between Jōzan and his garden over thirty years. Jōzan didn't sweep his own garden because he lacked a gardener, nor simply because "he loved cleanliness." It was because he felt an affection for each stone and clump of grass that no one else could know. All of the littlest and seemingly most insignificant objects of the garden were ruled by a complex hierarchy that was visible only to its creator. This hierarchy was impossible to explain to anyone else, and so subtle that any gardener, no matter how accomplished, would destroy it at his first touch. Jōzan had no choice but to sweep his own garden.

This was not the first time I walked through the gardens of the Shisendō. Nor were my visits restricted to the spring. But whatever the season, I always felt a certain peacefulness redolent of spring, a warmth, a relaxed atmosphere, a feeling of being at ease in a surrounding familiar to me, a sense of intimacy that touched the depth of my heart. There is nothing unusual about this architecture: it has no air of greatness; it is not overcharged with sentimentality, nor is it stern. It is naturally full of spring's warmth, as if it could not be otherwise, and with utter casualness the building stands there very firmly. Had its builder been searching intentionally for effect, the structure might never have achieved so strong a presence. What kind of person, or rather, what kind of spirit was responsible for this? The garden is very different from the famous imperial garden villa in Kyoto, the Shūgakuin, with its grandiose vistas, or from the cleverly designed garden of Katsura Detached Palace. It possesses nothing of the sternness of the Zen stone garden of Ryōanji, nor the absolute artistry of the Kohōan tea house garden at Daitokuji. But it has what those well-known gardens do not possess, a quality that cannot be separated from the fact that the Shisendō was the place of retirement and seclusion for a man who spent thirty years of his life here and who found in every plant and tree an ineffable, incalculable significance. The garden must have had incalculable significance to its creator, for if he had wished he could have gained power, accumulated wealth, and, with his renown as a poet, founded a poetry school of his own. Yet, according to the biography, "he remained unmarried all his life and avoided all conflict." Nothing was as important to him as a single plant or tree in the garden, and this attachment to every plant and tree must have been the reason he took up the broom himself—and why this garden is different from all others.

I was not used to walking for such a long time, and my legs were fatigued. After strolling through the garden once I returned to the main building. Trying to avoid the bright sunshine, I sat down on the verandah and, leaning against a pillar, stretched my legs out on the yellowish floor mats. I closed my eyes and heard in the distance the voices of the birds. There was no human sound; only the clack of the "deer-scarer" water mortar, a bamboo pipe that beat against the rock, breaking into my peaceful world at regular intervals. The sound of bamboo striking stone did not linger in the air. Like a short sharp fit of temper it was suddenly there, then suddenly gone. The intervals of silence were long, and just as I had forgotten the sound would return, it struck my ears again suddenly.

All this time my legs, stretched out on the mat, felt comfortable, but gradually I became aware of the hardness of the pillar against my back and I toyed with the idea of lying down full length on the mat. Too lazy to move, however, I remained in the same position while my ears registered the sounds of the birds that hopped from branch to branch, coming closer then fading again into the distance. Once more the verse came to mind:

At the deserted cloister, not a soul.
Noontime in spring, eternity.

And this verse brought out of my uncertain memory another of the master's verses:

Leading the life of a hermit, I am dedicated to nothing.
By nature disposed to be idle, I feel at ease in solitude.

The master of this retreat said of himself that he was living there without attachment to anything. This was not an unusual attitude. In fact it is commonplace and quite ordinary for a person living in retirement, East or West, then or now. But Ishikawa Jōzan was not an ordinary man. At the age of sixteen he received the patronage of Tokugawa Ieyasu and became proficient in the art of warfare. He won public recognition as master of the equestrian art, spear-fighting, and judo. After distinguishing himself in battle, this able samurai from Mikawa Province resigned from his post to dedicate himself to writing poetry. This was what led the famous Tokugawa poet Kan Chazan to remark that "Ishikawa Jōzan stands alone in his nobility." Jōzan's poems were well known, particularly in the Edo period. Kan Chazan was not the only poet of the time to make a pilgrimage to the Shisendō to pay poetic homage to the great Master. But does Jōzan's verse "By nature disposed to be idle, I feel at ease in solitude" suggest that had given up even the composition of poetry?

When I came to this point in my reflections, suddenly the bamboo pipe struck sharply against the rock again. The voices of the birds disappeared and there followed a moment of deep silence. The moment passed, and as I listened I could hear again the calls of birds, some near, some far. I took a deep breath. The three students had disappeared. Perhaps they were taking a rest in the shade of the trees or had already left the garden while I was not watching. In there place was an old man, sitting near me on the verandah looking into the garden. I wondered when he had come. Such a well-cared for garden would certainly require a gardener. If this old man was not the gardener, he might be someone from the neighborhood who visited from time to time. He wore casual Japanese dress, and the surroundings did not seem to interest him especially. After a while he turned to me and addressed me in a straightforward manner.

"Do you known anything about Jōzan?"

It would be a nuisance to hear the well-known story of Jōzan's life from the old man. I decided to forestall him by saying, "Yes, he is the Li Po or the Tu Fu of the Land of the Rising Sun." A Korean envoy is said to have uttered those words after he had seen some of Jōzan's Chinese poems. All the accounts of Jōzan mention this remark. I expected the old man to react with something like "It's rare for a young man nowadays to know such things," and I prepared myself for the rather dull conversation that would inevitably follow. My presentiments, however, proved to be wrong.

The old man's next remark gave our conversation an unexpected turn.

"Don't you think foreigners tend to exaggerate?"

He spoke in the same casual tone as before. I knew now that he was not the gardener. He might be a man from the neighborhood, and yet he did not look like that type of amateur historian who is dedicated to the study of local great men.

The old man continued, "Where are you from?" Without waiting for a reply, he went on. "When we are given a word of praise by a foreigner we are very pleased and carry it around like a talisman. It's the same today as it was long ago, don't you think?"

I thought how oversensitive Japanese society has become since our defeat in the war to the compliments and criticisms of foreigners with regard to Japanese culture. Nor was this sensitivity confined to culture—it reached from the lofty heights of foreign policy to the earthy depths of toilet design. But this was not what the old man meant. He was thinking about how, starting with the Zen priest-poets of the Five Temples, the Muromachi and Edo poets knew no greater honor than to be praised by the Chinese for producing poems "free of a Japanese odor."

"There is Japanese poetry and Chinese poetry. So long as you compose Chinese-style poems it is not at all strange that the ideal poem should be free of a Japanese smell; and the Chinese are the ones to decide whether a poem smells Japanese or not. This was the accepted view. But Jōzan paid no attention to this."

"Yet," I took up the argument, "the thirty-six poets he considered immortals were Chinese. He copied the works of Chinese poets. When he attempted to compose Chinese poems, he must have had his own ways of ridding his poems of a Japanese feeling."

"Those are not real poems," said the old man bluntly.

It occurred to me then that the old man's questions and answers had indicated from the beginning where the conversation would lead. I had made a bad start with my first remark. I shouldn't have said anything about the "Li Po or the Tu Fu of the Land of the Rising Sun." I don't know much about Chinese poetry. For a person like myself, who had never committed Li Po and Tu Fu to memory and who had never composed any poetry, it was dangerous to talk about what was and what was not a real poem. If Jōzan's poems were not real poems, then what were they?

"Just expressions of his ideas," I ventured somewhat vaguely.

"No, reminiscences," answered the old man promptly.

"Reminiscences don't necessarily take poetic form," I replied.

"That's why Jōzan wrote:

Composing poems, I grew old
But still I have not succeeded in stirring the hearts of the gods.

"To move heaven and earth and stir the hearts of the gods and spirits" was considered the supreme virtue of poetry in the great preface to the ancient Chinese classic, *The Book of Songs,* and the phrase had been adopted unchanged in the Chinese-language preface to the classical Japanese poetry anthology *The Collection of Japanese Poetry Ancient and Modern.* That much I knew. Jōzan says that he had not succeeded in stirring the hearts of the gods because he never found the perfect order to arrange his words in. Was he being modest? As I said, I know little of poetry. Still I rank Jōzan over Fujiwara no Seika and Hayashi Razan. Jōzan's poetry transcends the cliches of his time and approaches a kind of confession. He possesses the language and the emotional power to communicate the poet's feelings of that day and that hour, creating a mode of expression that is almost personal. That makes his work far more interesting to me than the fixed patterns of Razan's and Seika's poetry. He may not have succeeded in "stirring the hearts of the gods," but at least he had not adopted the conventional ideas of Seika or Razan as his standard.

"The thirty-six poetry immortals poets—they made the poetry," said the old man, "Since they made the poetry, all that was left Jōzan were reminiscences—Jōzan talking to himself."

I had already observed for some time that the old man never smiled. When you listened to him you had the feeling he was always smiling, but not the faintest trace of a smile crossed his face. What should have appeared as a smile did not show itself but simply cast a calm over his immovable features. The wrinkles around his eyes were deep. He might be in his mid-sixties. Small of build, he looked strong, even hardy. He might have been a craftsman once, perhaps involved in the discipline of some art, and retired from work, or, for all I could tell, not even yet retired. He was well informed about Jōzan, but his appearance was not that of an academic. I had already lost the natural opportunity to ask him his name, and now the conversation had reached the point where he had declared that Jōzan's poetry was simply an internal monologue. There was nothing I could do but go on with our discussion.

I was not prepared to accept his view that the composition of poetry was a sort of monologue. Especially when my partner was as self-assured as this. I tend not to readily trust those who are too self-assured. "Monologue will never result in a poem," I said. "If you write for yourself you need not worry about the rhyme, you need not even finish your sentence, like James Joyce when he wrote his famous interior monologues."

"You cast your monologue into poetic form. It's the trick of accomplishing that which gives you pleasure, don't you think?"

"In other words, it's the pleasure of speaking to an imagined partner."

"No, what Jōzan enjoyed was the process of making the poem. He didn't care about the completed poems. He didn't care whether they were read or not. He didn't need readers."

"Certainly, he may not have needed Seika, Razan, or the Korean envoy as an audience, but don't you think that he thought of the thirty-six poetry immortals as his imaginary audience?"

"Do you know the art of the spear-fight?" asked the old man suddenly.

I looked into his face. It bore the same self-assured expression as before.

"When you train yourself in the art of the spear-fight," he continued, "you don't need a partner. You practice until the point of the spear moves of itself in the direction of any target you choose."

"Yes," I acknowledged, "but in the case of the art of the spear-fight the partner, or target, is within the realm of physical space. You cannot apply this to the relationship between the form of a poem and its audience. You can practice the art of the spear-fight without a partner, but whether or not a poet can select words without thinking of an audience is a different matter."

"Why? If you eliminate the audience, the form of the poem remains."

"And where did that form come from?" I asked.

"The thirty-six poetry immortals."

"From the cultural tradition, you mean," I replied. "Culture is created by people. When Ishikawa Jōzan composed poems, wasn't he creating the culture of his age—at least a small part of it? To create poetry from a monologue is to take a monologue, to take the ramblings of James Joyce's hero, and to transform them into a cultural product. And because culture cannot be isolated from those who support it, the audience will always exist, even if it be an abstract one—that is, the reader as a bearer of culture. The composition of poems . . ."

"Was not his main concern," the old man interrupted me again.

"Then what was the main concern of Jōzan at the Shisendō?"

"To prepare tea by himself, drink it by himself; to make poetry by himself and read it by himself; to sweep the garden by himself and look at it by himself."

"And sweeping the garden was the same to him as composing poetry?"

"I'd rather say that sweeping the garden became the same as composing poetry."

The old man had gotten to his feet, so I also stood up, and when he started to walk I walked beside him. This happened naturally, and before I realized it we were following the small garden path in the direction of the valley. The sun was still high. There was no wind. The city of Kyoto was far off. Walking toward the valley seemed like walking toward the cries of the birds.

I listened to the old man's talk about Jōzan's sense of elegance. I could not completely accept what he said; retiring from the world and sweeping a garden was not my ideal. Yet Jōzan of the Shisendō seemed to come alive through the words of the old man. He knew far more of Jōzan than I did. Whoever he might be, there seemed to be no reason not to present him with the question I had long entertained about the reasons for Jōzan's retirement.

Jōzan's desire to retire from the world did not begin with the construction of the Shisendō at sixty. He earned glory in battle at the Osaka Summer Campaign by disobeying military orders and engaging the enemy in battle before the planned attack was to begin. He was disciplined for his disobedience and took Buddhist orders, retiring to Myoshinji when he was thirty-three. The next year he was offered a position in the service of Matsudaira Masatsuna, but he declined it. It's very likely that his courageous deed in battle and his violation of military orders canceled each other out, so that he was not prevented from finding a good position in some lord's service. Yet he took the initiative in actually rejecting a proffered post. Perhaps he did so because he was firmly committed to entering Buddhist orders. But one year later Jōzan made the acquaintance of Hayashi Razan and Fujiwara no Seika, and he abandoned Buddhism for Confucianism. Ogyu Sorai, in typical fashion, writes that "Jōzan abandoned Buddhism and adopted Confucianism, he gave up the military arts and practiced the literary arts." At any rate, Jōzan's commitment to Buddhism was slight enough that he was to give it up after only two years' practice.

Jōzan finally accepted a post at the age of forty-one, at Itakura Shigemasa's urging. In 1623 he went to Hiroshima to serve Asano Tajima no Kami. He did so to support his ailing mother; she died in 1635, and one year later Jōzan made his way back to Kyoto, never to return to Hiroshima. He was fifty-four. Until he retired to the Shisendō at fifty-eight, he continued to decline an offer to serve Itakura Shigemasa, refusing to rescind his original decision. Depending upon how you look at it, for nearly sixty years of his life, from thirty-three to ninety, Jōzan remained unwavering in his determination not to serve in public life—except for the thirteen years in Hiroshima to support his sick mother. If it wasn't a commitment to Buddhism or the ordinary impulse to retire, what was the reason for this determination? What could have spurred Jōzan to the point of violating military orders during the Osaka Summer Campaign?

"Well, you have to hear the whole story to understand that," said the old man.

And he proceeded to tell me, in his collected fashion, without the least hesitation or pause, which suggested to me that he had told this tale many times before.

Jōzan's father was a valiant samurai of the Warring States period. He decided to give young Jōzan lessons in spear fighting himself. He claimed allegiance with no school or method, except to declare that spears were not for thrusting but for killing. Each lesson continued until the opponent was as much dead as alive. No one in the fief came forward of their own accord to learn from him, but his son could not escape. Jōzan's father had little acquaintance with books. "You can't win battles with books," he'd say. The realm came to those who took it, and there was no need for the fussy reasoning of Confucianism to justify the rule of the victor. He was a great drinker, and when he was drunk he talked about the Battle of Sekigahara. His stipend was small. But that rarely bothered him. It bothered his wife far more. When Jōzan was sixteen, his father was suddenly struck down by illness. The terrifying spear-fighting lessons came to an end. The tyrant was dead. Jōzan couldn't help but feel a sense of relief. He was not filial to his father. His mother was not upset by her mismatched husband's passing. What he had not been able to do, she looked to Jōzan to achieve. When the official period of mourning was over, Jōzan entered service as a personal retainer of Tokugawa Ieyasu. Winning his master's favor, it looked as if he would make the most of this development. All that the son lacked to surpass his father was a military triumph, his own Sekigahara. And that's when the Osaka Summer Campaign began.

Ieyasu departed from Mikawa leading a large force, and the thirty-three-year-old Jōzan accompanied him. His mother said nothing to him, but he knew very well what her thoughts and hopes were. This was not only a chance to win acclaim in battle, but perhaps the last opportunity the son would have to prove himself his father's equal. To his mother, the Osaka Summer Campaign was a battle between father and son. Not only was this probably to be the last of the great battles, but the night before the battle, when Ieyasu had prohibited his personal retainers from engaging in any private confrontations as he waited for all his forces to gather, would probably be the very last opportunity for Jōzan to prove himself. After Ieyasu's advance guard had attacked the castle the next morning, there would be little opportunity to engage the enemy. If Jōzan followed orders and waited until the morning, he might earn a larger stipend than his father, but Jōzan's unbloodied spear would never have an opportunity to match his father's spear again. Yet if he disobeyed the order and went off to enemy territory on his own, his prospects were hardly better. Even if he returned alive, he might be sentenced to death for disobeying orders, or at best ordered to give up his offices and enter Buddhist orders. Only then, though, would his father be truly dead, and he a true samurai. Would he spend the rest of his life under his father's shadow, or die, now, as a samurai? Jōzan made his decision and secretly left Ieyasu's camp that night.

Jōzan attacked the enemy armed only with his spear. He came back with the head of one of the enemy samurai. Before that he had already killed two foot soldiers. His spear was indeed swift, but his opponent carried a sword, and he dealt Jōzan his share of wounds. Jōzan ignored his injuries and killed his opponent. With the head slung over his saddle he galloped, drenched in blood, back to his own camp, where he encountered Ieyasu's advance forces. Jōzan dismounted and announced himself. With that he had accomplished what he had set out to do. When the battle was over, rewards and punishments were declared, and Jōzan was ordered to shave his head and enter Buddhist orders at Myoshinji. He had been prepared for that from the start.

"Yes," I thought to myself, "in that battle with the spirit of his dead father, Jōzan had resolved his Oedipus complex, and had no more reason to remain a samurai." I was certain, though, that his decision to enter Buddhist orders was not made when he secretly left Ieyasu's camp, but only after his sentence had been pronounced. If that was so, there must have been some relationship between his experience of battle and his decision to become a monk. What was the relationship? Or was everything to be explained by Jōzan's complex?

"Have you ever killed anyone?" the old man asked suddenly.

"Of course not!"

"It is horrible," he murmured.

"I suppose in battle you're half-crazed, but when you realize what you've done . . . "

"On the contrary, a skillful spear man is never crazed. When Jōzan realized how many men he could kill, he realized the vanity of killing. But no, before that he knew the horror of the pleasure he felt as his arm moved swiftly through the air—moved mechanically, to stab and to kill."

"Wasn't it the enemy that was horrifying?"

"No, not the enemy," said the old man. "At that time he decided to throw away the spear and take up the brush. Do you know that a great Chinese painter once said 'one's will is in the tip of the brush'? The ultimate principle of the spear and the brush are one and the same."

Ishikawa Jōzan was a great master of the spear, just as he was a master of brush—so famous that in his later years he was praised by the emperor himself. Does the argument that perfection in all arts converges at a single point hold in this case? If it does, perhaps it was wise indeed to abandon the way of the spear, which moves of its own accord to destroy self and others, and take up instead the way of calligraphy and painting, placing one's will at the tip of the brush.

I was, however still not prepared to accept the old man's explanation of Jōzan's motives for giving up his military career.

"Is it not possible," I said, "assuming the Osaka Summer Campaign resulted from Ieyasu's intention to stage a surprise attack, and that false charges were advanced to justify the attack, that Jōzan, witnessing this dirty war, may have gotten sick and tired of politics?"

"There may be something there," answered the old man somewhat vaguely.

"But the difference between a dirty and a clean war is surely only a matter of degree." I countered. "War in any case is nothing but the extreme form of a struggle for power, and this is certainly not true only for the Osaka Summer Campaign. Wouldn't you say that the important thing about the Osaka Summer Campaign was not that it was a dirty war, but that there were no more wars afterwards, that it was the last battle upon which the two hundred and fifty years of peace of the Tokugawa were founded? How could Jōzan have reconciled in his heart his hatred of war with any regret for participating in a war that eliminated the possibility of future wars?"

"He had no regrets," said the old man.

"Well, then, let's call it disapproval. If he disapproved of war in general, how could he have disapproved of a war that eliminated war's possibility."

"The elimination of causes for future wars was not accomplished by the Osaka Summer Campaign," said the old man again.

I did not quite agree with this argument. Of course the security of the long years of Tokugawa political power was not only due to Ieyasu's destruction of the Toyotomi clan. But if he hadn't destroyed the Toyotomi, he could not have carried out his major reforms at the beginning of the Edo Period, such as the change of the feudal laws; the strict control placed over the samurai, the imperial household, and court nobles; the suppression of the Christians and so forth. It certainly seemed true that this would not have been the concern of Ishikawa Jōzan at the end of the Osaka Campaign, thirty-three at the time. When he decided to abandon his military career, what were his reasons, how did he justify his decision?

"When the war was over," I continued to reason, "and Ieyasu had died, social changes, based upon the dictates of the Tokugawa shogunate, were in the making all over the country. Under such circumstances the state should have had need of a talented man like Jōzan, even if he himself showed little ambition to embark on a successful public career. After so many years of warfare there must have been few samurai who were qualified to do administrative work, and fewer still who excelled Jōzan in intelligence. He should have been enlisted in the shogunate's administration for the sake of the public, if not for his own interests."

The old man gave no direct answer but muttered something and then diverted the conversation. "What is right before the war is considered criminal after the war. The prewar villains become the righteous afterwards. How can anyone know what is for the sake of the public?"

"If the battle of Sekigahara had turned out differently, the 'Heavenly Leader' Ieyasu would have been the outlaw?"

"Let us stop talking about political matters."

"Even if we stop talking about political matters they will continue to exist and shape our lives. Ignoring politics is just another form of political behavior. Jōzan's society needed his services because he was a talented man, and this situation would not be changed by Jōzan's resignation or his aversion to political matters. What about the Confucian motto 'Rule the country and pacify the world'?"

"It was Razan who said that. And Itakura. . . . "

"Itakura Shigemasa?

"No, Itakura Shigemune. But there was something that Itakura didn't understand," mumbled the old man again, as if to himself.

"He didn't understand poetry?" I asked.

"On the contrary, he understood poetry better than any other samurai."

The old man went on to tell how kindly Itakura Shigemune treated Ishikawa Jōzan. Both Shigemune and his brother Shigemasa were old friends of Jōzan. Their father Katsushige had been one of Ieyasu's personal retainers, serving as the city commissioner of Sumpu, then Edo, and finally the shogun's deputy in Kyoto. He died in 1624. The Itakura brothers were very well acquainted, from the inside, with the new government's policy on prisoners, which started with the release of prisoners in Kyoto in 1623 and gradually took shape as a national prison system by 1635. Jōzan served at Hiroshima from 1623 to 1635. Shigemasa urged him to accept the post, not only because he was concerned about Jōzan's financial straits but as a move to forestall any action that might be taken against Jōzan as the criminal record system was put into place. This was the beginning of the special concern of the Itakura brothers for Jōzan. Later Shigemasa took part in the Shimabara Uprising and was killed by Amagusa's forces. Shigemune inherited his father's role and became the shogun's deputy in Kyoto, making a name for himself as a sage judge and able administrator. In its difficulties with the nobility during its first years, the Tokugawa shogunate was fortunate indeed to find a man like Shigemune. Not only was he extremely able, he had the education and talent to exchange poems with the nobility, and his trips to the Shisendō were one of his great pleasures. But even for a man as cultivated as Shigemune, what placed Jōzan above the rank and file of Confucians was Jōzan's mastery and knowledge of spear fighting. Shigemasa understood the elegance that defined Jōzan's world. But he could not understand that Jōzan would place devotion to that elegance over the good of the nation. Shigemasa urged Jōzan to take a government post not for his own sake but for the sake of the nation, it is said. On that occasion Jōzan is supposed to have answered that the realm had no need of a man like him, and he had no need of the realm.

The old man seemed anxious to convince me of the validity of his argument. "In this world," he said, "it is common practice for a man to be called to do an important job, and then, when his work is done, to be thrown out again. There are countless examples since the battle of Sekigahara where people gave up everything for some cause, yet when they were no longer needed they were left without even a means of livelihood in their old age. Okubo Hikozaemon, so trusted by Tokugawa Ieyasu, was granted a fief of only two thousand measures of rice—and how many Okubos have died at Sekigahara and at the siege of Osaka and have simply been forgotten? For them nothing could have been worse than their fatal involvement in politics."

"Don't we live for some higher purpose?"

"Perhaps, but politics is not it."

"For Jōzan, wasn't the composition of poetry, in other words culture, just such a higher purpose?"

"'Past events are all an empty illusion.'"

"Did Jōzan at thirty-three not have a future?"

"If you live with worldly attachments, time passes quickly. It is never too early to decide to live without such attachments. The time at the Shisendō passed quietly. When time passes quietly . . . it forces you to come to terms with yourself instead of coming to terms with the world."

I could not help thinking that Ishikawa Jōzan must have been more thoroughly a misanthrope than I had first imagined. According to the old man, Jōzan, after his glory in battle, was not only horrified by himself but by the whole world as it had revealed itself during wartime. Politics knew no ideals, and so there was no reason to direct his idealism to political life. In fact, in his retirement Jōzan received only those of his friends who were poets. In spite of that, there was a time in his later years when he sought to leave the Shisendō and return to Mikawa. The reason was that he couldn't bear the steady stream of visitors, and he wanted to hide himself even farther afield in the countryside. This man who "never married and avoided conflict" first avoided women, then gradually cut off all contact with the world until finally he even tried to avoid communication with his fellow poets. How had this intense dislike for people originated? It seems to me that he must have avoided politics because he disliked people, and not vice versa. But Jōzan's avoidance of women probably preceded his experience at the Battle of Osaka when he was thirty-three. On this subject, the old man had not yet said a word.

Jōzan was sixteen when he went into mourning for his dead father. At that time the youth had a feeling of liberation from the father whom he had feared, and when the old man had spoken of a "lack of filial piety," his remarks may have been justified. Jōzan did, however, earn a reputation as a pious son—not toward his father but toward his mother. Behind Jōzan's decision to disobey orders and run off prematurely to battle in the Osaka Summer Campaign, the old man said, was his mother's silent wish. And his decision, after having given up his official post once, to take another in Hiroshima may not have been entirely to support his mother, as is usually thought. Nevertheless, it was certainly one important factor, and whatever else is said, Jōzan did cherish very special feelings for his mother. What kind of a person was this mother? The old man had not wasted many words on her. I imagined that unlike the tall, strong father she was of rather small stature, and in contrast to the father's coarse manner she must have been a gentle, refined lady with a taste for literature which her husband did not possess. These are my own musings. But if they were even partly so, it could explain that very special affection between mother and son. If this were so, the son was surely trying to find his mother in every woman he met, and he was doubtless already convinced before he tried that he could not experience with any other woman such love as existed between him and his mother. Perhaps Jōzan avoided women before he even knew them because of his relationship with his mother. Anyway, these were my thoughts.

The old man's story, however, was very different.

At the time when Jōzan worked as Ieyasu's personal retainer there was a maid of the inner chamber by the name of Taka. A letter which she wrote to Jōzan gives some clues about her personality. The letter was written in the simple Japanese syllabary, but the handwriting showed a strength that could only have been acquired by someone accustomed to writing Chinese characters as well. In it she wrote only of casual matters, yet through them she subtly hinted at her feelings for Jōzan. Taka was not an extraordinary beauty, nor did she have any particularly distinguished family background, but her wit, intelligence, and refined character were unusual. It was not customary for a maid of the inner chambers to write to a personal retainer of a feudal lord, and Jōzan did not answer the letter, though it moved him. At that time Jōzan was seventeen, Taka was twenty. Shortly after sending the letter, Taka obtained permission to return to her country to visit her sick father. Shiga, her home province, was not far from Mikawa. It was not a propitious time for a lady to travel alone, since the smoldering fires from the period of internal wars were not yet completely extinguished. Jōzan was ordered to escort her. When the party arrived in Shiga, however, her father's illness proved not to be serious— in fact, he was no longer sick at all.

What happened during this journey? The old man did not reveal the answer, but only muttered "women are devils."

After their return, Taka never saw Jōzan again. Two years passed. It was winter again when it happened that Taka's secret intimacy with a young page was disclosed and she was executed. The young page was a precocious, beautiful youth whom Jōzan had once loved. The boy must have been unaware of the full consequences of his actions. When their affair was exposed, Taka did not look ashamed at all. She went to the execution place composed and calm, lifting her face to the north wind whistling through the grove, barren of leaves at that time of year. The youth tried to escape, abandoning the woman to her fate, but he was caught. He was not allowed to plead for his life and after his beheading his corpse was publicly exposed. Only three days had passed since the execution of the woman.

This story of the old man seemed to me to explain everything. Jōzan, who did not approach women, had at least been in love with a boy. The lack of interest in the other sex, or perhaps the feeling of frustration, or even, the premonition of a feeling of frustration, made him look for an outlet in a relationship with the same sex. It lies within the nature of things that Jōzan, after his homosexual relationship had ended in agony and despair because of the interference of a woman, tended more and more to dislike people.

"You are very fond of explanations," said the old man.

"How else could you interpret this?"

"If you must have an explanation, you might say, he was trying to avoid encumbrances."

"Encumbrances! We are talking about women, who fortunately—as you said before—are devils."

The old man scrutinized me. "Fortunately?"

"Yes, fortunately, for one cannot taste fully the pleasures of this world without striking a bargain with the devil."

"The pleasures are short, but the encumbrances last."

"Do you mean that Jōzan never dreamt of women, or if you like, leaving aside women, never desired to experience pleasure with handsome boys? Did he not have a feeling of regret to have missed a great many of the pleasures of this world?"

"Well, the one or the other, what is the difference?" said the old man calmly. "Sodomy has the advantage of no subsequent complications. The Zen monks practiced it because it is easy to break ties of that kind when they become burdensome. The Monk Ikkyu was no good. He was no good because he got mixed up with women. First, Jōzan avoided women. Nor was he so foolish as to ruin himself by getting too involved with young men. If a feudal lord has descendants, family quarrels will flare up. What would have happened if Ishikawa Jōzan, who had only a small allowance as a samurai, had left descendants? How could he have expected to be treated with piety by his sons, when he himself had not shown piety toward his own father? As one gets older there is no end to the ailments of the body. It may be better to have no son than one without piety:"

Weak and sick I fear the wind and the dew
And wonder how I shall live through the fall.

I thought of Charles Darwin, who became sick after his famous voyage and, like Jōzan, at the age of thirty-three withdrew from the world—to a country house in Kent, where he lived for the remaining forty years of his life. Darwin had a very faithful, devoted wife. There exist two explanations concerning the nature of his illness. According to one, it was an organic disease caused by a kind of trypanosomiasis. According to the other, it was a psychogenic neurosis. Particularly if the latter were the case, he might not have been able to compete the work on his *On the Origin of Species,* which was published seventeen years after his withdrawal to the country house, had his wife not been there to help him. Jōzan had not been able to find a woman who could be his wife, but his case was to be attributed to his bad luck rather than to his wisdom.

"His upbringing," I said, "his surroundings, his first encounter with a woman, those were factors he could do nothing about. It was his fate. But if things happened as you related them, it is not strange that Jōzan should have avoided women."

"Young people like explanations nowadays," said the old man again. "But that's not how life works. As for Jōzan's reasoning, perhaps it was thus: if he had a faithful wife, he would be indebted to her; there is no greater encumbrance than indebtedness to a faithful wife. If she were unfaithful, he could kill her, but it is not easy to decide the life and death of a human being. Whether she was a good wife or not, whether he killed her or not, he would have difficulties. There was no better solution than not to take a wife."

"Wouldn't you say that he was too hasty in jumping to such a conclusion just because of his experience with one woman?"

"It does not follow that his conclusions would have been different, even had they been based on his experiences with three women instead of one. More is not always better. Heaven bestows experiences on us, and all we can do is to develop our ability to think and draw our own conclusions. There are good luck and bad luck, wise and foolish thoughts; we are helpless before fate, but responsible for our own thoughts. Insight is effective in good luck and in bad. Stupidity is just as evident in good luck and bad. The problem is not that Jōzan reached a conclusion after experience with one woman; if there is a problem, it must be that in that encounter Jōzan's intelligence failed him. If that is so, please tell me where in his encounter with that woman would you say that Jōzan's thinking was deficient?"

At this point the old man adopted an argumentative tone, as if he were defending Jōzan, and it was difficult for me to know if he spoke for himself or for Jōzan. He refused to budge from his position that women were demons and marriage was wrong.

"Anyway," I concluded, with a feeling of resignation, "he thoroughly hated women, and when in due time his hatred extended to all humanity, the Shisendō came to be."

"What an absurd idea," the old man retorted immediately, "the Shisendō was open to people."

It was not only the literati who frequented the Shisendō, explained the old man, but there was the gardener, and the old woman who was in charge of the kitchen, and, from time to time, people from the village came up too. They appealed to Jōzan to act as mediator in their disputes, and when the harvest was bad, old and young joined in a request to have their taxes reduced. The allowance of Jōzan in his late years, which he had been granted by the Tokugawa official Itakura Shigemune, was certainly not high, but with the very few expenses he had, he was able to either reduce the taxes or to make his own resources available for relief whenever he heard that the village people were in need. The story goes that when Jōzan died in 1672 at the age of ninety at the Shisendō, over a hundred villagers came to the funeral to pay their respects.

"Is it possible to call such a man a misanthrope?" The old man seemed very anxious to prove his point. "If a man avoids encumbrances," he added, "this does not imply that he hates mankind. On the contrary, in order not to hate people, it is necessary to keep them at a distance. Love and hate are two sides of a coin. If the bond of love is strong, hatred will also be fierce. This is true for the relationship between parent and child, and even more so between man and woman. The relationship of a wise man with his friends, however, is like water. He is on good terms with others without losing himself. If one is intimate with a woman, it is difficult not to lose oneself; if one has children, it will be difficult not to be blinded by love. This is the reason why Jōzan did not approach women, did not desire children."

"Certainly," I commented, "Jōzan was safe. No matter how close he came to the people of the village, the framework of Tokugawa society was never in danger of disruption. It was easy to preserve their superior-inferior relationship, and on Jōzan's part no need to worry that he would lose himself."

The old man did not seem to grasp my sarcasm.

I thought once more of the man who renounced the world at the age of thirty-three to write *On the Origin of Species,* which later changed the course of Western history. What had Jōzan, living in seclusion, contributed to Japanese history?

"Jōzan had no intention whatsoever to change the course of history," said the old man. "The Osaka Summer Campaign, the Shimabara Uprising, Ogyu Sorai's writings on the Chinese sages, Motoori Norinaga's studies of ancient Japanese texts—those are events without which history might have taken a different course. They are one thing. But to live the only life you have as your one and only life—that is quite another thing. The two can never be reconciled; if you chose one you forgo the other. Jōzan decided to live his own life. For Jōzan in his old age, grand historical achievements were not as important as living through one day of spring in idleness and peace at the Shisendō. If he had been prepared to sacrifice one single day, he might have made an impact on the course of history. But he was a man who would not spare that day. No matter how it might have changed the world thereafter, a day lost was lost forever, and even the publication of a work like *On the Origin of Species* would not have been an adequate recompense. Jōzan composed poetry. But he did not compose poetry for its own sake, he created poems only as long as doing so was a part of his daily life, just as he swept the garden as a part of that life. At Shisendō Jōzan had no intent to create anything. He was only trying to live after his own fashion," was how the old man explained it.

But Jōzan lived thirty years after retiring to the Shisendō. Granted that Jōzan had no ambition to participate in worldly affairs and possessed no desire for women, but hadn't he even been tempted by the idea of traveling? Didn't the news of the Shimabara Uprising alarm him?

"No, everything was there at the Shisendō," said the old man. In the daytime he enjoyed calligraphy, and when he got tired of writing, he swept the lanes of the garden, reciting his favorite poems to the groves and the streams. At night he read old books, and at the fireplace he sometimes mixed herbs to make ointments and medicine for his own use. When he was hungry he baked sweet potatoes. The seasons brought continuous changes to the forested slopes of Higashiyama. There were nightingales in the spring, the voices of the deer in the fall, the sound of the rain on the roof in the summer, the wind blowing through the pine trees of the nearby mountain in the winter . . . the golden leaves of an autumn evening were different every year, and the grass beneath the trees was new every spring."

Listening to the old man I felt as if I were living through the seasons at the Shisendō. I imagined the bubbling sound of the boiling water in the kettle, the smell of the fire-logs, the softly falling snow in the night, the humid warm wind and bright sunshine reflected on the surface of the water in the early spring, the fast movement of the summer clouds, and the smell of the earth at the beginning of an evening shower. I imagined all the seasons which came and passed away over the trees, the water and the stones of the garden as if I experienced them myself. Was the garden designed to stimulate my imagination, or was I charmed by the words of the old man as he talked of Jōzan's daily life?

"It existed only once, it disappeared, and it will never return," I sighed.

"Yes, we only live once," said the old man.

"Jōzan, however, made this garden. And his garden is still here."

It was such an effortless creation, in perfect harmony with the land and the passing of the seasons. There was no exaggeration, no surprises in the garden; you could visit it and stroll through it again and again and never be bored. The effect it produced was far more subtle than any calculated effect could ever hope to be. All perfect creations are a spiritual testament. I said before that I liked Jōzan's poetry. Now I saw that his garden could by no means be ranked lower than those designed by the great Kobori Enshu. The unobtrusive arrangement of stones, the open skies, the delicate curves and the gentle ups and downs of the small paths, surprisingly open clearings among the trees, the skillful placement of *clairière*.

"Yes, the garden is still here," said the old man, "but it has nothing to do with Jōzan any more. Jōzan is dead."

Jōzan had lived here almost three hundred years ago. I recalled the seven verses that Okubo Shibutsu had written one hundred fifty years after Jōzan's death. Two verses are preceded by the remark, "On the occasion of a visit to the Shisendō one hundred fifty years after Jōzan's death." One of them reads:

Vermillion gates may rise and fall,
    pieces on a chessboard!
Unlike this thatch-roofed hut,
    which goes on for all time.
A hundred fifty years ago
    seems just like yesterday;
Daylight wind and clear night moon:
    always, the same book-curtains.[1]

If you only replaced "one hundred fifty" with "three hundred," the ode was a perfect description of my own feelings. Of course, unlike Shibutsi, I am inept and lacking any gift, and my visit to the Shisendō produced not even a single verse, against his seven. I am tainted by my attachments to worldly matters, and though I have no confidence in what it is I am here to accomplish, I know that I lack the decisiveness to abandon my livelihood, give myself up to country life, and, like Jōzan, never cross the Kamo River again.

Jōzan lived as he wished. What became of him after death?

"In death we return to nature," concluded the old man with a calm detachment.

Suddenly I thought I heard the sound of the "deer-scarer" water mortar striking against the rock again. I looked around, but the old man had disappeared. I stood up and stepped out into the garden, where the tress were throwing long shadows on the grass, though the sun seemed far from setting. The faint noise of streetcars came up from the distant city of Kyoto.

Translated by Hilda Kato,
revised by Jeffrey Hunter

1. Translated by Jonathan Chaves.

PLATES

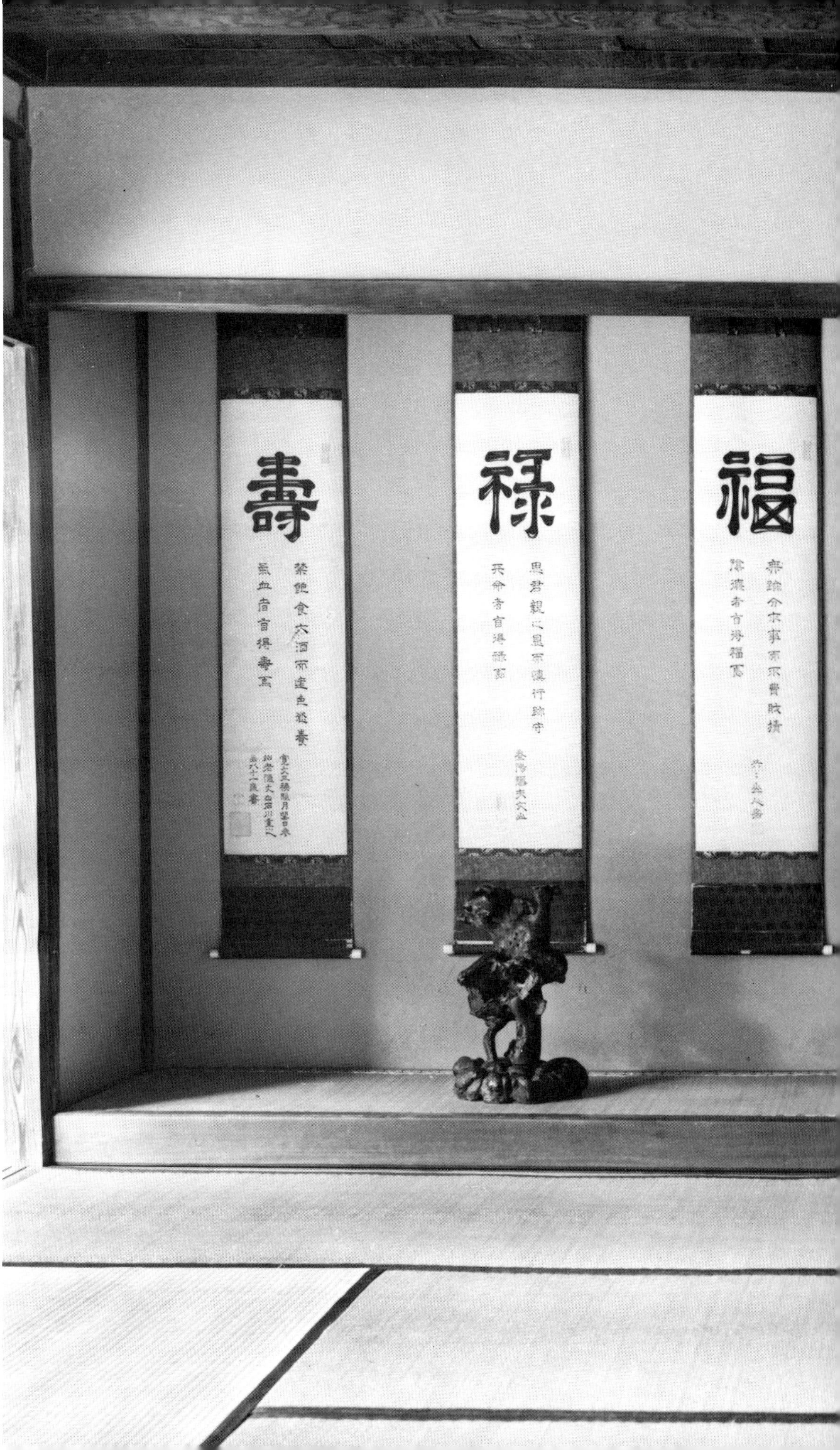
壽
祿
福

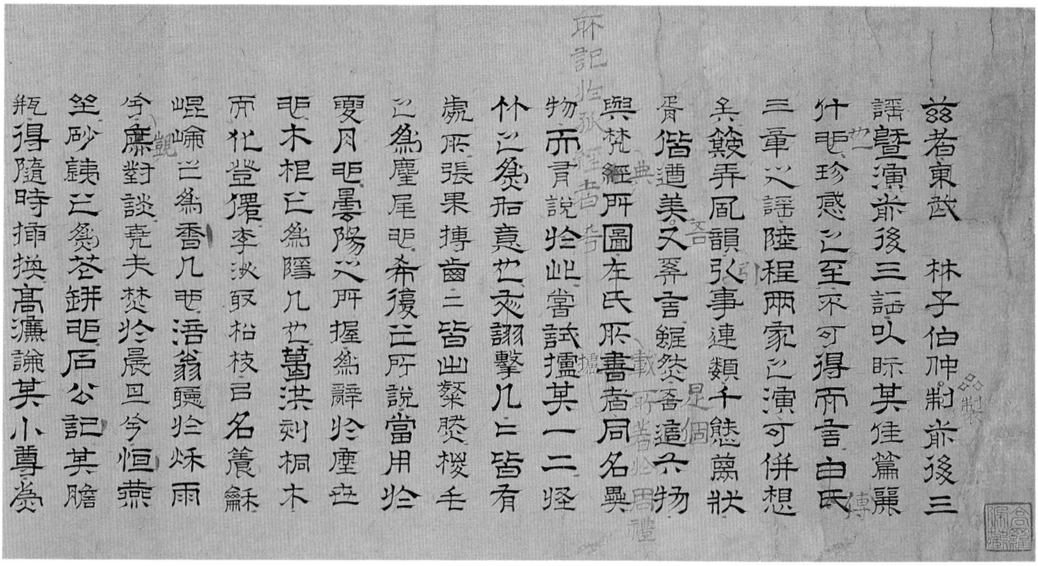

茲者東武　林子伯仲制前後三
謠暨演前後三話以眎其佳篇彙
什也珍感之至不可得而言由氏
三章之謠陸程兩家之演可併想
矣較弄風韻引事連類千態萬狀
胥皆適美又弄言鯹然畨適亦物
與梵經所圖左氏所書者同名異
物而肯說於此嘗試攄其一二烴
竹之爲柄意也爰謝擊几上皆有
號所張果搏齒之皆出棃駁櫻毛
之爲麈尾也希復之所說當用於
夏月也曇陽之所握爲辭於塵世
也木榻之爲隱几也葛洪刻桐木
而化登僊李泌取松枝以名養穌
崐崘之爲香几也浯翁聽於烁雨
兮熏對談堯夫焚於晨旦兮恒燕
坐砂銚之爲茗餅也石公記其贍
瓶得隨時掃換高濂論其小尊彝

別昆崇
骨肉縁枝
葉結交亦
相因以涙
皆兄崇誰
憂行路人
況我連枝
封舁子同
一言苞憂鴛舁
舊今秊參舁辰

蘇武

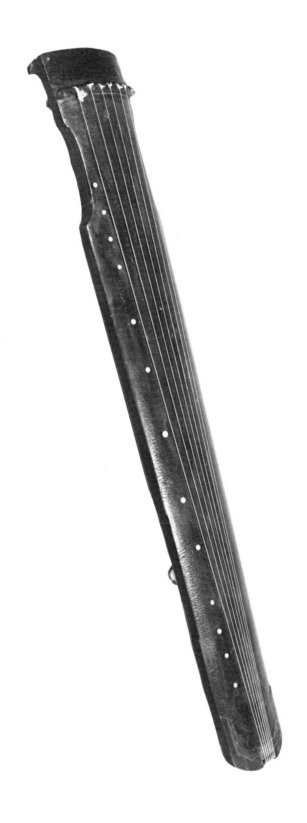

視驢言為

客亶大寂混合陰

陽先生天地柔剛

漢丞相諸葛亮書

建寧二年三月

辛卯朔七日乙

酉宫杜

臣

晨

長

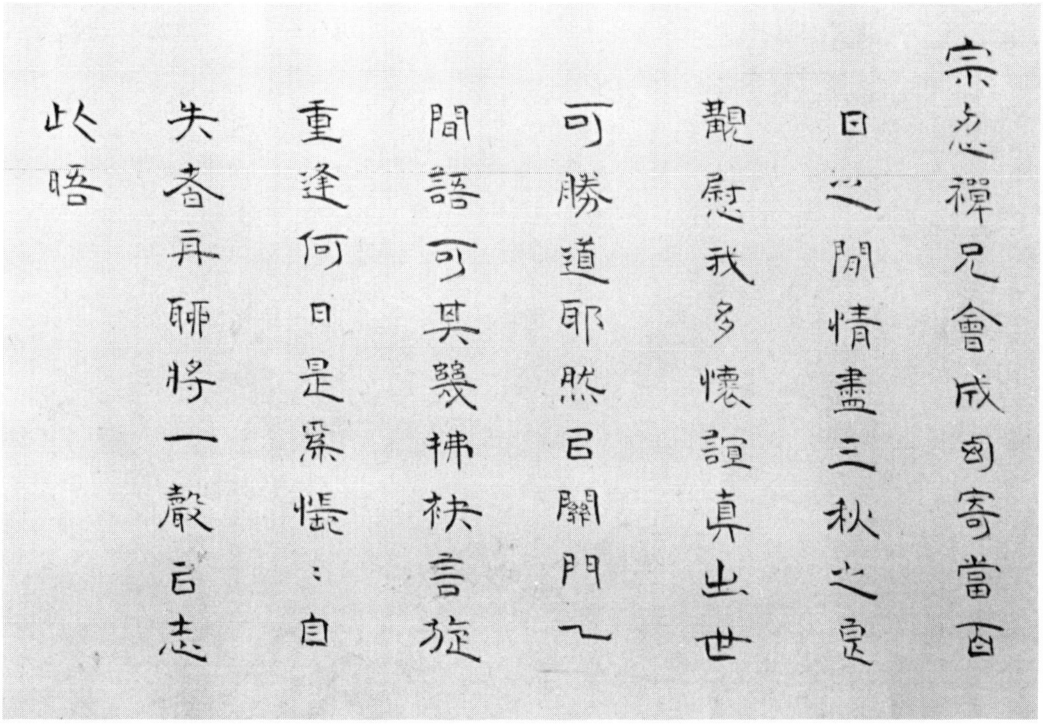

宗忞禪兄會成句寄當百

日之閒情盡三秋之思

覿慰我多懷誼真出世

可勝道耶照已關門一

間語可其發拂袂言旋

重逢何日是慕慰：自

失杳无聊將一敍云志

此晤

189

梁皇殿上不戩緘唇
怒合杭津直坐安心
已竟乙苓五葉栗替
東皁越杜多寫賞

詩儷圖說

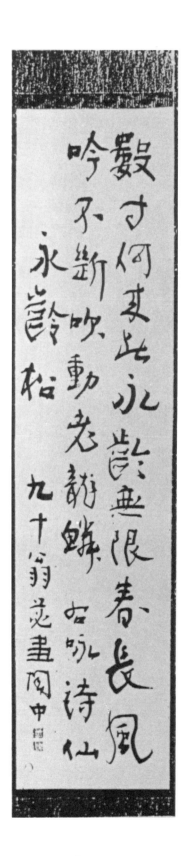

毅寸何支比永齡無限春長風
吟不斷吹動老龍蜂好咏詩仙
永齡松

九十翁光亮盡閻中

194

詩仙堂記

詩仙堂為何而作也
石川丈人為避世以遊而作也
丈人若奉州泉莊産而果世
士林巴嘗仕
大神君嘗過不鯉余之為遊也
每暇日讀書賦詩自励氣義
乙卯之俊千令先登於難波城
櫻門刻擊斬獲以顯其名及
大神君振猿之日而後　丈人不出
而善仕　先毋以衰之遊事藝
陽者有年矣至於杯圈口澤之
氣存馬抛毛義之織乃来洛陽
相攸於台麓一東寺遍伐惡
木削奧州決疏旧知搜剔山鄉
新肯堂揭中華詩人三十六
輩之小影於壁上寫其詩各一
首於側號曰詩仙堂余在東武
與丈人詩筒手書千里面譚
其論詩仙歎笑登来冬余
因官命入洛會其来問共喜殊
甚一日幸應炤景之　招与春齋
同往　丈人從後迎之郎入衡茅
到其堂直升其樓滴一路之空
翠洗九陌之市紅快武振衣名
岳則杉嵐晴而自舍輝濯足鴉
河則水月流而殖淀清西矚鳳城
仰王澤之来謁南望鳩嶺敬神
感之如在四宮阿原之豆五方也

山中有流水借問不知名
映地為天色飛空作雨聲
轉來深澗滿分出小池平
恬澹無人見年年長自清
參陽文□老□

朱子家訓

父之所貴者慈也子之所貴者孝也君之所貴者仁也臣之所貴者忠也兄之所貴者友也弟之所貴者恭也夫之所貴者和也婦之所貴者柔也事師長貴乎禮也交朋友貴乎信也見老者敬之見幼者愛之有德者年雖下於我我必尊之不肖者年雖高於我我必遠之慎勿談人之短切勿矜己之長讎將以義解之怨者以直報之人有小過含容而忍之人有大過以理而諭之勿以善小而不為勿以惡小而為之人有惡則掩之人有善則揚之處公無私讎治家無私法勿損人而利己勿妒賢而嫉能勿逞忿而報橫逆勿非理而害物命見不義之財勿取遇合理之事則從詩書不可不學禮義不可不知子孫不可不教奴僕不可不恤守我者理也聽我之命者天也人能如是天必相之此乃日用常行之道若衣服之於身體若飲食之於口腹不可一日無也可不慎哉

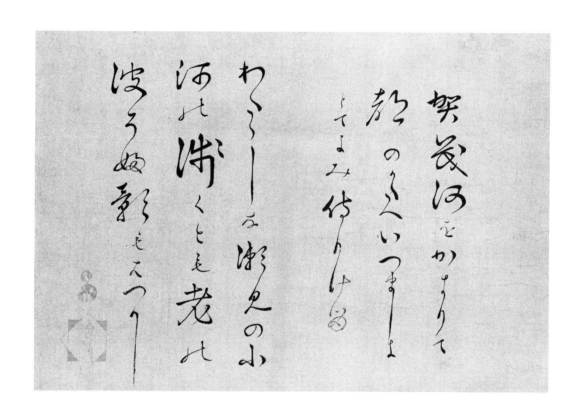

契茂河をかへりて

船のうへにつよよみ侍りける

わゝしる瀬見の小

河せ洗くとも老せ

波う々ぬ影をぞつ

鴨河長漲

萬古一條水淩清不耐舟
遠逖台水出近傍洛東漎
分派通雷社納涼傾希州
何心詠歌太息贊在河洲

洛陽晚煙

風煙寰宇間決皆弄歸摛
斜影三千文肆塵十萬家
浮𡮾凝物色連地罩京華
幾訳從危竈細縕尊紫霞

僧都詩并序

爰有僧都也古今集中載汰田僧都自
器名之添水添田者耕

古賀益昌由来者漸洵聲矣有栢竹吃哉山為田僧野自水
器耳顏片石聲韻轉旋搞揮首餘於上田下短野稻興水自
俗微歌起鳴声於春曉俞係山空凡佇發矯尺巨石流下水
鼓声尾旎旎片石聲韻轉旋搞揮首諸亮如
已起鳴声於春曉俞係山空苦傳響通無晝與稻興
喚時鴍鹿逐子亦屋蕚益隱興空苦傳響通無心生
田時蟹出蕚不駛出家歐作寒吃喉禮生
目出不遲曲也潛出田歐歐作寒吃喉禮
霹吃吹吹色山層秋守野倒澗流水滿覆嵩
足鼓潤自鳴形側守田有聲荅山阜萠
爾吃憂後為誠乢澗流水有
石出憓削六六必人四
宿里怡

六六必人四

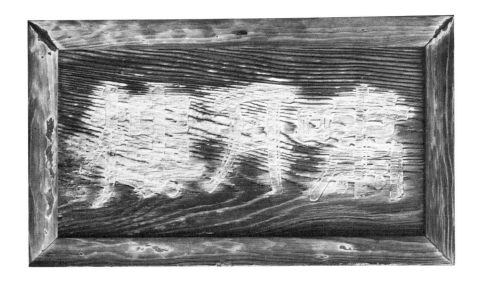

詩仙堂

Captions

Numbers refer to the pages on which the illustrations are found. Unless otherwise noted, all works of art are in the possession of the Shisendō.

137. The approach to the Shisendō complex.

138. The stone steps leading up to the Old Plum Gate.

139 The Old Plum Gate with its calligraphic plaque.

140. The stone pathway leading to the Entrance Hall.

141. (*Above*) The courtyard in front of the Buddha Hall. (*Below*) The window of the Buddha Hall.

142. The roof of the living quarters.

143. A view of the Tower for Whistling at the Moon from the east.

144. The southern façade of the Tower for Whistling at the Moon.

145. A window in the second story of the Tower for Whistling at the Moon.

146. Stairs leading to the Tower for Whistling at the Moon.

147. The ceiling of the Tower for Whistling at the Moon, with its calligraphic plaque.

148–49. The tokonoma (ornamental alcove) in the study, with several calligraphy scrolls by Ishikawa Jōzan.

150–51. A view of the fore garden from the study.

152. A side view of the fore garden.

153. A view of the fore garden from the Hall of the Poetry Immortals, the paintings of the Chinese poets visible beneath the ceiling of the hall.

154. (*Above*) The rustic ceiling of the Hall of the Poetry Immortals with its portraits. (*Below*) The circular window of the Tower for Whistling at the Moon.

155. The roof of the study with the Tower for Whistling at the Moon.

156. The fore garden with a miniature Chinese pagoda.

157. The Waterfall for Washing Away Ignorance.

158–59. A general view of the roof of the Shisendō.

160. The miniature Chinese pagoda emerges from mounds of azaleas.

161. The pruned azalea hedge below the fore garden.

162. (*Above*) Morning light on the white sand. (*Below*) Stone steps.

163. The Tower for Whistling at the Moon beneath the light of the full moon.

164. A stone lantern and the small garden pavilion.

165. Clouds over the bamboo garden.

166–67. The lower garden.

168. Path to the garden pavilion with a bamboo fence.

169. The outer gate with a calligraphic plaque.

170–71. A general view of the Shisendō.

172–73. A view of the thatched roof of the main hall and the garden, with an ancient persimmon tree heavy with its autumn fruit.

174–75. A view of the fore garden from the study.

176. Fallen maple leaves and the water mortar.

177. A Camellia in the garden.

178–79. Snowscape from the garden pavilion.

180. Ishikawa Jōzan, *Draft Manuscript* (detail), private collection. This section of a handscroll that Jōzan wrote for the two sons of his friend Hayashi Razan shows Jōzan changing his text at times, and at other times changing the way in which he wrote a character for aesthetic reasons. This handscroll therefore gives us a rare look at Jōzan in the midst of his artistic process.

181. Kanō Tan'yū (1602–74), *Portrait of Jōzan,* private collection. Jōzan and Tan'yū seem to have been friends for many years. Tan'yū's portrait of Jōzan, therefore, is born of deep knowledge of his subject.

182. Ishikawa Jōzan, *Virtue Plaque,* private collection. The formal beauty of Jōzan's clerical-script calligraphy is especially suited to plaques and signboards. This indoor plaque is made of wood and inlaid with mother-of-pearl.

183. Kanō Tan'yū, *Portrait of Li Ho.* Although it is now very weathered and worn, this portrait of an immortal Chinese poet by Tan'yū gives us a sense of the beauty of the original set of paintings that Jōzan commissioned and inscribed to hang at the Shisendō.

184. Kobayakawa Shūsei, *Portrait of Su Wu.* After the original set of paintings by Tan'yū had become too weathered, another set of paintings was commissioned from the twentieth-century painter Shūsei, and it is this set that now hangs in the Shisendō.

185. Jōzan's *Ch'in.* The *ch'in* is a seven-string zither that for the past two thousand years has been beloved by Chinese (and later, Japanese) literati. It has a deep and soft tone that is particularly suited to playing alone or for a friend, and listening to the music of the *ch'in* is considered a way to quiet and harmonize the mind.

186. Ishikawa Jōzan, *See, Hear, Talk, Move,* Kyoto Mingeikan. These four characters form the opening of a calligraphic handscroll by Jōzan. He wrote each of the characters in a different form of calligraphy, moving from standard to clerical to running to cursive scripts. The text is the *Four Admonishments* of the eleventh-century literatus Ch'eng Yi.

187. Chu-ko Liang (181–234), *Calligraphy Rubbing,* Tokyo University Library. Although some later critics have argued that Jōzan only saw later examples of Chinese calligraphy in clerical script, he wrote that he much admired this example of fourteen characters by the famous Han-dynasty military strategist Chu-ko Liang.

188. Han dynasty, *Stele of Shih Ch'en, 169 A.D.,* private collection. This stele is famous because the anonymous calligraphy in clerical script is considered among the finest examples of Han-dynasty writing.

189. Ōbaku Dokuryū (1596–1672), *Poem in Clerical Script,* private collection. Dokuryū (Chinese: Tu Li) was a Chinese poet and calligrapher who came to Japan in 1653 and became a monk of the Ōbaku Zen sect. His use of clerical script is very relaxed, modest, and informal.

190. Tōkō Shin'etsu (1639–96), *Poem on Portrait of Daruma,* private collection. Shin'etsu (Chinese: Hsin-yueh) was a Chinese monk of the Sōtō Sect who emigrated to Japan in 1677. He became famous in Japan not only as a monk but also as a painter, calligrapher, poet, seal-carver, and musician on the *ch'in.* His use of clerical script is more elegant and formal than that of Dokuryū.

191. (*Above*) Ishikawa Jōzan, *Large-scale Clerical Script.* When Jōzan wrote large clerical script he utilized the "flying white" technique, allowing the paper to show through the brush strokes. The formal design and balance of his characters is also exceptional. (*Below*) Ishikawa Jōzan, *Plum Gate.* When one climbs the second set of stairs leading to the Shisendō, there is a rustic gate with a signboard reading "Plum Gate" carved from calligraphy by Jōzan. This signboard, although now quite weathered, is all the more beautiful for its perfectly balanced calligraphy and aura of age.

192. Ishikawa Jōzan, *Single-line Calligraphy.* Although Jōzan customarily wrote in clerical script, this impetuous and dramatic calligraphy is in "wild cursive" style and demonstrates the artist's complete command of the brush. The text reads, "It still is like a burning house," a passage from the Lotus Sutra.

193. Ōbaku Monchū (1739–1829), *The Ageless Pine at Shisendō,* private collection. Monchū, a Japanese monk of the Ōbaku sect, lived at the Shisendō

when he was ninety years old (by Japanese count) and wrote this poem at the time.

194. *Wooden Statue of Ishikawa Jōzan*. The statue of Jōzan preserved at the Shisendō shows us the poet at an advanced age, leaning on his arm rest and perhaps chanting a poem.

195. *Painting of Su Wu*. This painting on a wooden door is of the immortal Chinese poet Su Wu watching two geese fly past. It is one of the few remains from Momoyama Castle now preserved at the Shisendō.

196. (*Above*) Hayashi Razan (1583–1657), *Shisendō Record*. This record of the Shisendō was written by Jōzan's great friend, the Confucian scholar Hayashi Razan. (*Below*) Ishikawa Jōzan, *Song of the Six Treasured Objects*. This elegant and forceful example of Jōzan's large-scale clerical script refers to six of his favorite treasures: a bamboo sceptor (*nyoi*), a fly whisk, a low-slung reading desk, a mountain-shaped incense burner, a metal flower vase recovered from the seashore, and a *chin,* or zither.

197. Ishikawa Jōzan, *Amid the Mountains*. Jōzan's smaller-scale clerical script maintains a sense of symmetry and balance that is enlivened by the modulations of line in the brush strokes moving downward to the left and right.

198. Ishikawa Jōzan, *The Family Precepts of Master Chu*. Master Chu, or Chu Hsi (1130–1200), was the founder and leading thinker of the Neo-Confucian School of Principle.

199. Ishikawa Jōzan, *Waka Poem*. Although Jōzan almost always wrote in Chinese, he occasionally composed Japanese poetry in the classical *waka* form. The calligraphy, appropriately, is much more fluid and graceful than his Chinese-style writing. This poem was supposedly written on an occasion when Jōzan declined an invitation from the emperor to leave the Shisendō and visit Kyoto:

"As I was considering crossing the Kamo River and making my way to the capital, I composed the following poem.

Alas, I am ashamed to cross it—
Though only a shallow stream,
It would mirror my wrinkled age."

The translation of the poem is taken from Howard Hibbett's translation of Jun'ichirō Tanizaki's *Seven Japanese Tales* (New York: Knopf, 1963, reprinted Putnam, 1981), 102.

200. *Two Views of the Shisendō.* These two views with poetic inscriptions by Jōzan represent (*above*) "The Long Flow of the Kamo River" and (*below*) "Evening Mist over the Capital."

201. Tomioka Tessai (1836–1924), *Poem on the Water Mortar with Preface.* This text by Jōzan was written out by the scholar-artist Tessai and then carved in wood. It is preserved at the Shisendō.

202–7. Ishikawa Jōzan, signboards and plaques. Jōzan's bold and elegant calligraphy was particularly well suited to carving onto signboards and plaques, and the Shisendō is graced with a number of them in various sizes and shapes. They can be hung indoors and outdoors to harmonize with the view. *Page 202, above:* "Hunger and Illness"; *below:* the writing is effaced. *Page 203, above:* "Shisendō; *center:* "The Lesser Paradise Cave"; *below:* "Wasp's Waist." *Page 204, right to left:* a couplet reading, "The bamboo gate descends to Primal Ground / The Plum Gate leans against the abbot's quarters." *Page 205, above:* "Gate"; *below:* "Transformation" (sign for the privy). *Page 206, above:* "Inscription of the Six Don'ts"; *below:* "Sated."; *Page 207, above:* "Troupe-l'oeil Nest"; *center:* "The Tower for Whistling at the Moon"; *below:* "Shrine of Auspicious Immortals."

208. The Shisendō, illustrated on a page from the woodblock-printed *Miyako Meisho Zue*, 1786. Griffis Collection, Wason Library, Cornell University.

About the Authors

Thomas Rimer is a professor of Japanese literature at the University of Pittsburgh. He has a wide variety of interests in many aspects of Japanese literature and culture and has written on both traditional and modern art, theater, and literature. His translations include the treatises of Zeami and the historical stories of Mori Ogai.

Jonathan Chaves is professor of Chinese at The George Washington University. He has published books and articles on Chinese poetry, poetic theory, and the relationships between poetry, calligraphy, and painting in China, as well as his own poetry. His book *Pilgrim of the Clouds* (Weatherhill, 1978) was nominated for The National Book Award.

Stephen Addiss is a professor of Art History and Humanities at the University of Kansas. A pupil of John Cage, he has composed chamber and vocal music, written extensively about Japanese art history and other subjects, and is also active as a brush painter and a calligrapher. His most recent book is *The Art of Zen*.

Hiroyuki Suzuki is a professor of Architecture at Tokyo University and one of Japan's leading writers on architecture, gardens, and crafts. In English he has published *Contemporary Architecture of Japan: 1958–84* (1985).

The "weathermark" identifies this book as a production of Weatherhill, Inc., publishers of fine books on Asia and the Pacific. Supervising editor: Jeffrey Hunter. Book design and typography: Liz Trovato. Production Supervision: Bill Rose. Composition: Trufont Typographers, Hicksville, New York. Color separations: ISCOA, Arlington, Virginia. Printing and binding: Arcata Graphics/Halliday, Plympton, Massachusetts. The typeface used is Berkeley Old Style Book.